REKINDLING COMMUNITY

Schumacher Briefing No. 15

REKINDLING COMMUNITY

Connecting People, Environment and Spirituality

Alastair McIntosh

with Case Studies edited by Sam Harrison
from WWF-CHE Scholars

Published by Green Books
for The Schumacher Society

First published in 2008
by Green Books Ltd
Dartington Space, Dartington Hall, Totnes, Devon TQ9 6EN
www.greenbooks.co.uk

for The Schumacher Society
The CREATE Centre, Smeaton Road, Bristol BS1 6XN
www.schumacher.org.uk admin@schumacher.org.uk

Reprinted 2012

Front cover photo: Eigg islanders symbolically walk ashore on the day of their
community land buyout, 12 June 1997. Most prominent are Maggie Fyffe and
behind her Karen Helliwell, then secretaries of the Eigg Trust and the Residents'
Association respectively. This photo and also the back cover photo of the author
by generous courtesy of Murdo Macleod of *The Guardian.*

The commissioned illustrations (Plates 1-8) are being placed in the public domain
– "Copyleft"– so that they may be freely used and adapted by readers for any
life-giving purpose. Versions including animated Powerpoint can be found on this
book's webpage: www.AlastairMcIntosh.com/rekindlingcommunity.htm.

Printed by TJ International Ltd, Padstow, Cornwall, UK

A catalogue record for this publication is available from the British Library

ISBN 978 1 900322 38 6

The Schumacher Briefings
Series Editor: Stephen Powell
Founding Editor: Herbert Girardet

Contents

Key to boxes in the text

(Named individuals are the WWF-CHE scholars. They have provided the photos from various sources. The picture of Colin Macleod used in Box 5 is by generous courtesy of Andy Sewell.)

Box 1:   *A Nation Built on Community* (Extract from the Papua New Guinea constitution)

Box 2:   Isabel Soria Garcia – *Holy Island of Arran: a sacred natural site where spirituality links people and nature*

Box 3:   Jamie Whittle – *White River: a journey up and down the River Findhorn*

Box 4:   From Papua New Guinea's *Liklik Buk*

Box 5:   Chris Adams – *Helping 'Fight or Flight' Take Wing: for Colin Macleod of the GalGael Trust*

Box 6:   *GalGael poetry from 'Fight or Flight'*

Box 7:   Brian Thom McQuade – *The Cycle of Regeneration: a study of urban community in Govan*

Box 8:   Sam Harrison – *Grounded Philosophy and the Practice of Wisdom*

Box 9:   Rutger Henneman – *The Spirituality and Theology of Scotland's Modern Land Reform*

Box 10:   Chriss Bull – *Women's Identity, Boarding School and Land Ownership*

Box 11:   Iain MacKinnon – *Lost Leaders: issues of change and identity in a Highland community*

Box 12:   Sibongile Pradhan – *Regeneration beyond Land Reform: deeper engagement with community and place in the women of Eigg*

Box 13:   *Manifestos of the Eigg community land trust*

Box 14:   Mike Price – *Meta-motivations and Micro-enterprise under Community Land Tenure*

Box 15:   Osbert Lancaster – *Values and Legitimacy: responsible purchasing at the Scottish parliament*

Box 16:   Samantha Graham – *Awakening to the Bigger Picture: epiphanies that result in corporate responsibility initiatives*

Box 17:   Wayne Visser – *Work in Sustainability as a Path to Meaning: values and self-transcendence*

For my son, Adam McIntosh,
who lives and thereby
teaches community

About the author

Alastair McIntosh was raised on the Isle of Lewis and is best known for his work that advanced land reform on the Isle of Eigg and helped stop the proposed Harris superquarry in a National Scenic Area. He is Visiting Professor of Human Ecology at the Department of Geography and Sociology, University of Strathclyde, and holds honorary fellowships at the Academy for Irish Cultural Heritages at the University of Ulster, the Schumacher Society and the Centre for Human Ecology (where he teaches on its acclaimed master's programme).

His books include the bestselling *Soil and Soul: People Versus Corporate Power* (Aurum 2001), collected poetry in *Love and Revolution* (Luath 2006), and *Hell and High Water: Climate Change, Hope and the Human Condition* (Birlinn 2008). His writing has been described by George Monbiot as "world-changing", by the Bishop of Liverpool as "life-changing", by Starhawk as "wonderful and inspiring" and by Thom Yorke of *Radiohead* as "truly mental".

A Quaker of the radical 17th century Ranter tendency and of interfaith disposition, he has worked for the Schumacher-inspired South Pacific Appropriate Technology Foundation in Papua New Guinea, for the Iona Community, and for a variety of community and academic organisations. Many of his scholarly papers and other contributions are online at www.alastairmcintosh.com, where there is also a webpage supporting this Schumacher Briefing.

Foreword

by Jean-Paul Jeanrenaud
Director Corporate Relations, WWF International

I was really delighted when Alastair asked me to write a few words for this Schumacher Briefing. In my youth I was also inspired by *Small is Beautiful*, and to this day continue to be uplifted by Fritz Schumacher's vision of a world in which capital serves humanity instead of humanity being enslaved by capital; a world in which people and nature co-exist harmoniously.

Alastair is a thinker and writer in the same tradition, a man of compassion and integrity whose spiritual ideals shine like a beacon in the darkness of this materialistic age. And I believe that, like Schumacher, Alastair is helping to describe and unfold a more holistic worldview.

The old industrial-capitalist-reductionist worldview is no longer adequate for our needs, and a new paradigm is emerging, because in the words of the poet T. S. Eliot, we ". . . are no longer at ease in the old dispensation." In fact we are increasingly dis-eased by our over-consumption and the consequent environmental and social decline that is spreading rapidly around the world.

So, can we expect this new dispensation any time soon? Yes, it is already beginning to take shape in our midst, but we must not be complacent. We are at a crossroads, and we must take individual responsibility to consciously nurture this new beginning.

It should be clear that although in one sense we are only a part of the web of life, we are also co-weavers. Whatever action we take shapes and reshapes the world we live in. The challenge is to ensure that our actions are benign and of benefit to all.

If we take up this challenge, the new paradigm will be an expression of a transformed way of being, based on compassion and understanding, and founded on mutual respect. Respect for the Earth, respect for each other and for different ways of seeing and being. It will be further strengthened through collaboration, partnership, and a shared vision aimed at building the 'fullness of community' that Alastair believes is ". . . the only hope both for the dignity of the human condition and for our co-evolution with Earth."

The Earth will once again provide for the needs of all, humans and nature, not just for the few who enrich themselves at the expense of nature and the rest of humanity. We will celebrate natural diversity and embrace a plurality of cultural and spiritual meanings.

Because we express our being, in and through nature, the current state of the planet reflects the impoverishment of the human psyche that has lost its sense of wonder and awe. It no longer sees the 'Great Spirit' both concealed and revealed in the natural world.

From the standpoint of Schumacher's *Buddhist Economics* the eco-logical crisis we are experiencing today is a rather predictable outcome of the kinds of deluded human behaviour the Buddha described 2,500 years ago. Greed, hatred and ignorance, the three poisons the Buddha spoke of, are now so widespread that we are quite literally poisoning the seas, the air, the earth itself.

Thus, the imperative of the present era is to *BE* rather than to *DO*. In order to *DO BETTER* we must *BE MORE*. This is not a justification for passivity and inaction; rather it is a call for the intensification of action, but at an interior level. It is a call for interior transformation and growth. This is not referring to external, physical 'Limits to Growth' but rather to the potential for limitless, interior, spiritual expansion.

To hasten this transformation and renewal we have to focus less on the outer and more on the inner work. This is the paradox of action. For ideas precede intelligent action. So, if our thinking is *Holistic, Healthy and Holy*, then our resulting actions will bring about positive change. It is surely more than just coincidence that holistic, healthy and holy, all have a common etymology.

As Kabilsingh puts it: "Only when we understand the true nature lying within can we live harmoniously with the rest of the natural world."

Through the transformation and growth of our inner being and the liberation of the hidden Self, outer renewal will occur. As Alastair puts it: "Self-realisation is not rocket science. It's just about getting real. Become yourself. Be yourself! Draw forth the same in others."

Introduction

Between 2005 and 2008 I held a research grant through Scotland's Centre for Human Ecology (CHE) from WWF International in Geneva. It was to support a team – mainly CHE fellows and our students who study in partnership with the Department of Geography and Sociology at Strathclyde University – to research the *spirituality* of rural and urban regeneration. We wanted to explore inner aspects of strengthening the bond that connects people, place and nature.

This Schumacher Briefing presents our findings. It profiles 13 pieces of research, each written up by the WWF-CHE scholar who carried it out. Around these I have woven a narrative that shares my own evolving understanding of the psychospiritual underpinnings of community. In so doing, I define spirituality as that which gives life, and specifically, life as love made manifest. That said, no intellectual definition of the spiritual can ever be wholly satisfying. Here we touch on the ineffable. For while spirituality can enlighten the mind, cognition can never reciprocally fathom the depths of Spirit.

For the most part this is not a book that deals with the nuts and bolts of community. Rather, it attempts to get to the foundations – what it can mean to discover community at the heart of humanity. My colleagues and I have left a thousand questions unanswered; after all, we had only a hundred pages. And we embody a spectrum of positions that range from socialism to advanced capitalism. But what unites these contributions is that they all seek soul.

Because this is a *Schumacher Briefing*, I have taken as my touchstone passages drawn from E. F. Schumacher's iconic *Small is Beautiful*. As different editions have varying pagination, I have referenced by the page number from my 1974 edition,[1] preceded by chapter number. For example, 9:131, means chapter 9, page 131. I have left Schumacher's original language untouched, though it is likely that a man of his empathy writing today would have used where he could gender-inclusive language.

In *Chapter 1*, I describe how my own understanding of community evolved when sent as a young man to Papua New Guinea to engage with appropriate technology as influenced by Schumacher.

Chapter 2 explores Schumacher's insight that the troubles of our times are "metaphysical", by which he meant, spiritual.

Chapter 3 examines what being human can mean, and how the Cycle of Belonging strengthens our interaction in community.

Chapter 4 focuses on the Rubric of Regeneration with rural examples of how spirituality can draw people and land into becoming communities of place.

Chapter 5 explores "economics as if people mattered", using fundamental human needs to examine both urban deprivation and corporate social responsibility.

A number of the ideas probed in this book – especially those on nihilism, essentialism and belonging – draw from a short thesis that I presented in 2008 to the Academy for Irish Cultural Heritages at the University of Ulster for the award of PhD by published works. Details are on my website, and I am profoundly grateful to Professors Ulrich Kockel, John Gillespie, Máiréad Nic Craith and Michael Cronin for their supervision, challenges, examining, and warm support. It goes without saying that the views expressed in this study are not necessarily the position of organisations or people with which it is associated, including WWF.

I am grateful to Sam Harrison who did a great job of editing the contributions by his fellow WWF-CHE scholars and pointing me towards eminently quotable material. Also, very warm thanks for the voluntary guidance of the Schumacher Briefings' commissioning editor Stephen Powell of the Gaia Coach Institute, and to John Elford at Green Books in admiration of his dedicated attention to detail. As for my wife, Vérène Nicolas, her presence runs as filigree through this work.

Lastly, I am truly grateful to Jean-Paul Jeanrenaud at WWF International in Switzerland and his former colleague, Luc Giraud-Guigues. Their interest and trust in providing resources on behalf of the world's largest conservation organisation made this research with my student-colleagues possible. It has allowed us to explore and share how human nature and wild nature can be harmonised from a perspective of deep grounding in life. My involvement with the *Strategies for Change programme* of WWF UK has also factored in to this.[2] The overall results point towards the possibility of a fullness of community in which, I believe, rests the only hope both for the dignity of the human condition and for our co-evolution with Earth.

Chapter 1

Towards a Becoming Existence

The Depth of Schumacher's Vision

It was in 1977 that I first read E. F. Schumacher's *Small is Beautiful*. I found it mindblowing. No wonder it quickly sold a million copies.

As I sat down to write this book I read it again, 35 years after its publication in 1973. This time I had a question in mind. I wanted to know what Ernst Friedrich, or 'Fritz' Schumacher, had said about *community*. I wasn't bothered with what he may have written elsewhere. It was his masterpiece that interested me, because that was what had resonated so richly with the wider and underlying *zeitgeist*, or spirit of the times.

It turned out that he had mentioned community quite often, but only in passing. But that's deceptive, for the whole book implicitly oozes it! What's more, Schumacher wasn't on about just any old sort of community. As he saw it, our relationship to one another and with this Earth is bound up with the deepest roots of what it means to be human. His vision drew from a soil – a ground of being – that, time after time in *Small is Beautiful*, is expressed in terms overtly *spiritual*.

It thrilled me to rediscover this. After all, if you ask people today what E. F. Schumacher stood for, most would probably not talk about the spiritual underpinning of global community dynamics! Instead, they might remember that he was a humane but sensible economist, a protégé of Keynes, who cut his teeth during 20 years with the National Coal Board. They will recall that he advanced the concept of 'intermediate technology' – an idea that became elevated to the almost prosaic realms of motherhood and apple pie. And they might add that he said something about "Buddhist economics . . . as if people mattered" – which kind of sounds like a nice right-on idea from the 60s, even if nobody's quite sure how 'practical' it would have been in practice.

And that's my point in writing this little book. We now need to deepen our collective understanding, and re-examine some of

Schumacher's insights in today's context of weakening social cohesion, disconnection from the land, ongoing wars and new threats to humanity – especially climate change. I might have missed a trick, but my sense is that the full depth of Schumacher's *Small is Beautiful* vision has not yet been widely understood, let alone built upon. His book may have been around since 1973, but the contents of its deepest treasure vaults have yet to be drawn into the sunshine.

This book is in part an attempt so to do. It's not that I'm an obsessive follower of Schumacher. I'm simply somebody who likes to respect – to re-spect – which means, to take a deeper look, at what some of our cultural elders have to say. It is my experience that when we honour visionaries and tradition-bearers, our own inner doors open more widely. Such is the magic of gratitude. The capacity to express it becomes a gift back to ourselves. We then start to see and receive things that would previously have escaped notice. At least, that's been my general experience, and it has been so in re-reading *Small is Beautiful*.

Intermediate and Appropriate Technology

Let me, then, start with the context in which I first encountered Fritz Schumacher's thought. I was just 22 at the time, and had been posted by Voluntary Service Overseas (VSO) to Papua New Guinea (PNG). It was a journey that was to draw me into the world of 'intermediate' or, as it soon came to be known in preference, 'appropriate' technology. The name shift from IT to AT is minor but significant. 'Intermediate' suggests a half-way house between low and high technology. The danger is that it can be seen as implying second best. What we need as human beings is neither low nor high technology, small nor big, but that which is most fitting in the service of giving life. The reality is that, sometimes, high technology can be the most fitting. Solar panels, or transistorised electronic governors for micro-hydroelectricity generating units, are good examples. That's why most practitioners soon decided that AT was a more suitable way of describing things than IT. Both terms capture the same spirit that pioneers like Schumacher intended, but AT is more flexible.

AT also leaves open a recognition that, sometimes, small in a literal sense is not the only way of being beautiful. For example, if Europe wanted to harvest bountiful solar energy in partnership with nations of the Sahara Desert and thereby tackle global warming, hi-tech AT on a pretty massive physical scale would be called for. When Schumacher spoke of "small" I don't think that he meant small-minded or Heath Robinson. He meant ways of living that fit to the rhythms and cycles of human beings and of nature. He specified that "small is beautiful" means technological development in "a direction that shall lead it back to the real needs of man, and that also means: *to the actual size of man*" (10:155, his emphasis). In other words, it implies a way of life that leaves people feeling empowered rather than disconnected and apathetic. It means technologies that humanise and draw us into relationship with the ecology of the Earth rather than ones that dehumanise and distance us from that relationship.

VSO had sent me to PNG supposedly to teach maths and science. I ended up as the deputy head of a school that we had yet to build, and which aimed to provide training for so-called 'drop-out' youths. These were village children who had 'failed' to get a place in a high school and, from there, a life in the city. They wanted to be educated beyond their present primary level, but destiny was pointing them back to the village. Our school – St Peter's Extension School – was set up by Archbishop Virgil Copas of the Catholic Church, together with four Mother Teresa Missionaries of Charity nuns. Coming from the highly Presbyterian Isle of Lewis in Scotland's Outer Hebrides, and in the early days of my own somewhat alternative spiritual journey, it was a weird but wonderful situation to step into.

Our role as teachers was to provide an 'extension' to the young-sters' basic education – one that would be aimed at helping them to enrich village life. The relevance of AT will be clear, though it has to be admitted that we were severely constrained in teaching it – not just by lack of resources but also, in my own case, by a marked deficiency of talent.

This became clear the first time that I set the students a multiple choice examination. It was my (very) basic mechanics class. The class average scored at precisely what one would expect from random guess-ing! Clearly, my talk and chalk approach was not going to do the job. I'd started off standing there describing, for example, the four-stroke cycle of an internal combustion engine. I'd be using such conventional language as *induction* – when the piston first moves down, drawing in the fuel and air; *compression* – when it comes back up, constricting the mixture; *ignition* – when the piston is forced down by the explosion, thereby giving the power stroke; and *exhaust* – as it lastly rises back up again, pushing out the waste gases. But I soon learned that the same could be introduced much more graphically, memorably and with a rollicking good laugh in the class by animating the cycle in such highly technical terms as "suck, squeeze, bang, blow"! They'll never forget it now . . . and neither, I suspect, will my reader.

I also had to learn to teach using what was all around us. The trick, wherever possible, was to demonstrate by doing – just like back home on any croft in the village. So it was that with an occasional fizzle, flash and jolt, I got the kids up ladders doing the electrical wiring of their own classrooms. That's the great thing about coming from a crofting community – one that lives at least partly from, and wholly with, the land and sea, like on Lewis. You pick up all sorts of skills without fully realising it. I knew the rudiments of how to wire things up, so I dug from where I stood and that's what we started off doing. It was tremendous fun and nobody got killed.

This led on to my being asked to do the electrical engineering on two micro-hydro power schemes in the nearby mountains. The confidence that gave to me as a young man really helped to draw me into my own power – a bit big-headedly at first, but that's all part of the young man's learning. Eventually, after returning to Scotland and acquiring an MBA to make myself more useful in the world, I went back to PNG in 1984 as a financial advisor. This time it was for two years with the Schumacher-inspired South Pacific Appropriate Technology Foundation (SPATF).

Here the work touched on everything from a scrap metal foundry run on waste oil to water pump manufacture, food processing technologies, village-based empowerment workshops and distributing the celebrated *Liklik Buk* of rural development.[3] Most famous of all was our 'Wokabaut Somil'. This portable sawmill, along with a forest management training programme, gave villagers an incentive not to allow the commercial loggers onto their land.[4] In all this we were frequently in touch with what was then called the Intermediate Technology Development Group (now called Practical Action) in England, and with similar Schumacher-inspired offshoots worldwide.

SPATF's visionary Papua New Guinean director, the late Andrew Kauleni, placed strong emphasis on the idea that AT was not just about technical 'hardware', but also, the human 'software'. People – their dignity, identity and place – are the primary and primal issues. This lay at the heart of PNG's 'new nation' constitution, summed up as "integral human development" – a rubric borrowed from liberation theology (*Box 1*). This whole heady mix would later have a huge influence on my own work with empowerment, human ecology and land reform back in Scotland. Some of its implications are summed up by a few lines from one of SPATF's then Board members, the Melanesian philosopher Bernard Narokobi.[5] Andrew Kauleni had these pasted up on his office wall. As I remember, they went something like this:

> Welcome to the University.
> The ancient, timeless, eternal
> University of Melanesia.
> The village,
> where courses are offered in living.

But for all that it sounds idyllic, life in PNG was also challenging. As a T-shirt that we used to wear put it, "Ho hum – another shitty day in Paradise!" My legs still bear scars from deep tropical ulcers. I have special fillings at the base of some teeth as a result of slight malnutrition. And I'm no use as a blood donor from often having had malaria. I also learned what it's like to be robbed and to have my life threatened. Yet, in spite of all that, I loved almost every moment of it. That was because the very nature of the place gave a context which constantly pulled life back into perspective. Day after day when I was based around Kerema in the Gulf Province, I'd end my work by just sitting back in amazement and gazing out to the distance. There, beyond all the hubris of human affairs – beyond even the mangrove swamps where we'd go to set our fishing nets – rose range upon range of mountains. They reposed there like Bernard Narokobi's Melanesian villages that they enfolded – ancient, timeless, eternal – silhouetted in mystical greens and blues, building one upon the other in tiers, an amphitheatre of the gods.

Simply to soak them in after a fraught day was enough. Like gazing at a starry sky, it reset reality into a proper cosmological context. Verdant forest veiled even the most towering summits. They made me think of *Obscured by Clouds*, the Pink Floyd soundtrack to an

Box 1: *A nation built on community*

from the PREAMBLE to the
CONSTITUTION of THE INDEPENDENT
STATE OF PAPUA NEW GUINEA, 1975

By authority of our inherent right as ancient, free and independent peoples

WE, THE PEOPLE, do now establish this sovereign nation and declare ourselves, under the guiding hand of God, to be the Independent State of Papua New Guinea.

AND WE ASSERT, by virtue of that authority

- that all power belongs to the people – acting through their duly elected representatives

- that respect for the dignity of the individual and community interdependence are basic principles of our society

- that we guard with our lives our national identity, integrity and self respect

- that we reject violence and seek consensus as a means of solving our common problems

- that our national wealth, won by honest, hard work be equitably shared by all.

Box 1: *A nation built on community (continued)*

NATIONAL GOALS AND DIRECTIVE PRINCIPLES

WE HEREBY PROCLAIM the following aims as our National Goals:

1. Integral human development

We declare our first goal to be for every person to be dynamically involved in the process of freeing himself or herself from every form of domination or oppression so that each man or woman will have the opportunity to develop as a whole person in relationship with others.

---

obscure 1972 French movie where a diplomat's wife discovers the meaning of life amongst the New Guinea tribes of a lost mountain valley. That regenerative capacity is what makes the wild matter. That's what plays mischief in the mind with such Western constructs as 'savage' and 'civilised'.

How very strange. We often want to get away and join their way of life; they, likewise, with ours. But little did any of us know what the future was to hold. Little did we suspect that, within a decade, this environment would become the target of revving chainsaws and surging bulldozers as the commercial logging companies started to move in.

My young man's honeymoon with life was to prove short-lived and my work embarked upon a darker phase. Soon I was to realise that nowhere on the planet is any longer beyond the reach of greed and the extractive power of technology. If it's not the loggers, it will be the mining company, or out at sea the industrial fishing ships that hoover up everything in the ocean.

Fritz Schumacher was merely one step ahead of the game. He could see the movements of the compass being pulled by the magnetic distortion of modern times. His prophetic eye knew how to, as I've heard

Hebridean people say, "watch all points of the come-to-pass." That was why he wrote his book for us.

Lessons from the Beast of the East

Small is Beautiful was one of several 'bibles' that I had taken in my minimal luggage allowance when I'd first headed off for PNG. But a disturbing thing had happened on that outbound plane journey in 1977. It was a trivial event in the great scheme of things, yet it has stayed with and niggled me . . . a sign of the times . . . a quivering of the needle of the come-to-pass.

Our cohort of outgoing VSO volunteers was block-booked together. We were on a scheduled flight from London to Sydney, and it had a reputation for getting later and later at every stop. A seasoned traveller told me they called it "the Beast of the East".

Our particular tussle with the Beast commenced at check-in. Our VSO trainers had hinted that it was usually possible to get away with a few kilos of excess baggage. Since we were all going to be away from home for two years, pretty well everyone took their chances, stuffing as much as they could into their rucksacks. But one poor guy drew the short straw at check-in. His baggage was no heavier than the rest, but an example was made of him. He got stung for £30 excess. In those days that was a lot of money. It counted as a week's wages for most of us.

In my Hebridean home community there would never have been any question about what to do. Somebody would naturally take it upon themselves to organise a whip-round. They wouldn't feel especially virtuous about so doing and they wouldn't be discouraged out of a misplaced fear of being thought 'goody goody'. They'd just be undertaking what everybody understood to be the done thing. So it was that I passed round an envelope – if I might dignify an airline sick bag as such – amongst our cortege of 20 or so travellers. Many hands could make light the loss. And after all, was our guilt not shared in common?

At first everyone seemed happy to contribute. The envelope went from hand to hand and was filling up nicely. Such is 'companionship' – the sharing together of 'bread' as from the French word, *pain*. But then the Beast of the East struck.

"Why should *we* pay for *his* excess baggage?" sounded a voice from the back of the plane. And this chap didn't just want to opt himself out. He wanted the comfort of carrying with him a following! To my dismayed astonishment, a handful joined the rebellion. The gesture still went ahead, but now it was somehow poisoned.

There's a lesson in here about community development. The voice of the 'saboteur' often speaks for others silent in the group dynamic. Each voice needs to be understood as reflecting something of the nature of the whole. On reflection decades later, I drew from this what I'll call my five lessons from the Beast of the East. I'd presumed:

... that community existed in ways it did not;
... a coherent congruence of group values;
... that my cultural norms were theirs;
... a legitimacy to act that was lacking;
... and to proceed without consultation.

Wow! Talk of beating oneself up! But that's the kind of critical self-awareness or 'reflexivity' that's needed if we are to rekindle community without getting burnt to an emotional cinder in the process. To be honest, I'm not sure that I'd do it any differently today. Sometimes – like when you're literally or metaphorically constrained to rows of airline seats – the opportunity to adhere to due process is limited. Sometimes you have to discern what's fitting to a given situation – participative democracy, representative democracy, or just assuming leadership in a presumption of authority – like when having cause to shout out – "FIRE!"

Long Green Tentacles

The key to working with others, as I remember one of our VSO trainers saying, is discernment. Discernment is the practice of seeking insight through sensitive awareness – perhaps even an inner seeing or 'scrying' of reality. I vividly remember the trainer's words. He'd said: "When you arrive at your postings, you'll need long green tentacles."

But a balance must be struck in all of this. Many right-on organisations get so tangled in the tentacles of process that they forget about the task they're supposed to serve. Such groups wallow indulgently in the sticky doldrums of their own unresolved neuroses. At the end of the day, our challenge is to discern and apply the appropriate mix of task and process orientation. That's what singles out healthy and productive organisations from sickly and sluggish ones.

Box 2: Isabel Soria García

Holy Island of Arran: a sacred natural site where spirituality links people and nature

My Research

The aim of this research was to understand what the spiritual value of nature might be for our society. This spiritual underpinning is germane to conserving nature in many cultures, however in the technologically developed world it doesn't rank highly as an element of resource management. I worked on Holy Island, which lies off the Isle of Arran in western Scotland. It is a place sacred to Christians, and more recently, Buddhists. I developed social methods of research, particularly drawing upon action research. The conclusions I came to were supported by in-depth interviews conducted with members of the island's communities which were aimed at gaining a sense of people's experiences in nature.

My Findings

The main conclusion that I drew from the research is that a spiritual view of nature is able to meaningfully contribute to our self-identity. Nature provides us with the possibility of experiencing our completeness as human beings. This generates a deep interconnection between people and nature which works reciprocally: spiritual practice helps you to experience nature, and vice versa. Nature therefore appears to be the most suitable environment to get to know one's innermost self. Feeling at one with nature creates a knowledge of interconnection that changes our behaviour. Encouraging the spiritual development of people will therefore contribute to nature conservation. Equally, the spiritual journey will be more complete in a well conserved environment where the sacred is easily recognised.

Box 2: Isabel Soria García *(continued)*

I concluded that spiritual values are a key but under-recognised element, reflecting our transcendental connection to nature and perhaps shaping our attitudes towards it. Spirituality therefore ought to be granted its place in informing our actions to manage nature. As such, Holy Island is an important source of 'spiritual power' for influencing 'right relationships' in conservation management. It is therefore important to build upon the status of this Sacred Natural Site and to support people's spiritual relationship to it in a manner that integrates with formal technical management tools. In so doing it will open a path for nature to teach us about ourselves and so help to achieve total conservation management.

Next Steps

After my research on Holy Island I became a formal member of the Task Force on the Cultural and Spiritual Values of Protected Areas (CSVPA) within the World Commission on Protected Areas (WCPA) of the World Conservation Union (IUCN). In the CSVPA I worked with the Delos Initiative. This works in several sacred natural sites from technologically developed parts of the world in order to analyse whether the spiritual values of a site are compatible with its natural values, and thereby create synergies.

Recently, within the Delos Initiative I developed a spiritually based management plan for a Buddhist monastery included in a Spanish protected area. The plan for this was presented in the 4th World Conservation Congress that took place in Barcelona in 2008.

My work conducted as a WWF-CHE scholar has been published as Isabel Soria, 'Holy Island, Isle of Arran', *Protected Areas and Spirituality: Proceedings of the First Workshop of the Delos Initiative – Montserrat 2006*, IUCN World Commission on Protected Areas, Gland, 2008, pp.218-234.

If we imagine a simple graph with task orientation running up the Y axis and process along the X, then the name of the game is to maximise the area of the triangle that can be shaded in if a line is drawn connecting the points. Some types of organisations are stunted because they focus too much on tasks. Here the brash and avaricious can hide behind the imperatives of hitting targets, maximising profits and ticking off performance indicators. Other types of organisation are stunted because they're strong on process but weak on task. Here the indolent and incompetent can hide behind exaggerated people issues, a grandiose sense of entitlement and obstinate insistence on due process to an extent that gets in the way of the job being done.

As a generalisation, commercial organisations are guilty of the first sin and voluntary ones, of the second. The delicious irony is that both are roads to Hell. Failure to attend to one dimension eventually undermines the other! The name of the game, therefore, is to push out the boundary on each axis simultaneously so as to maximise the area shaded. It seems obvious. But as George Macleod, who founded the Iona Community, was fond of saying, we too easily forget that "God is never served by inefficiency."

Equally, as old George said on another occasion, we forget that "Only a demanding common task builds community." An organisation that is a mere money-making machine can find social coherence as a narrow community of interest. There's nothing surprising about that any more than there is in honour amongst thieves. But to have community in a sense that expands what it means to be human and to live sustainably on this Earth requires very much more than being a mere community of interest. It needs a shared life-affirming vision. And that requires its people to have a certain congruence of values even though the process of discerning what that is means tolerating, and indeed, valuing, being a community of contested discourses.

Meanwhile . . . if we might step back into the belly of the Beast of the East . . . a majority of my fellow travellers had, notwithstanding the objection of one amongst our number, contributed to the collection. But as we saw, this breakdown in group solidarity soured the gesture. It left me feeling like an interfering do-gooder. No longer was I simply passing an 'envelope'. It had reverted, veritably and dismally, back to the sick bag! Probably I was being over-sensitive. Giving and the ego are usually more closely bound than we care to confess. But culturally I felt wrong-footed, rather as a fish out of water. It's said that culture is like that. You don't see it when you're in it because your whole life moves there. It's not until somebody pulls the plug and the pond drains that you realise what you've just lost.

So it was that the Beast of the East was one experience amongst many that taught me, wiser but sadder, that the principles of community are neither obvious nor desirable to everyone. The everyday practicalities of it all can be simple, indeed, elegantly humble. That's made clear in the wonderful illustration 'How to Build Community' that I have included in this book, courtesy of the Syracuse Cultural Workers in America.[6] And yet, the very need for such a poster comes about because, in today's world, we don't all swim in the same pond. We cannot take for granted either a sense of community itself, or even, people's basic notion of what it means. And community cannot be rekindled on assertions of goodwill alone. We move in times when, in the view of many and as Mrs Thatcher famously told *Women's Own* (though arguably taken unfairly out of context), "There is no such thing as society. There are individual men and women, and there are families."[7] That presents us with a huge challenge. If we want to believe that there is, or at least, can be, such a thing as society, then we need to argue a persuasive case capable of opening up closed hearts. That's the work of rekindling community.

There is a challenging asymmetry in all this. Individualism can prosper when it is riding on the back of community. But community cannot prosper when selfish expressions of individualism take advantage of it. Capitalism, now writ large onto the fabric of our world, therefore 'succeeds' because it openly embodies a relentless dog-eat-dog logic, the bottom line of which is violence. Ironically, communism fails because it attempts to resolve the asymmetry just mentioned by coercion – the bottom line of which is also violence. Either way, violence wins, and that's why the world is in a mess.

That's also why our search for community must push beyond the conventional polarity of capitalism and communism. The limitation of both of these is that they make 'man' the measure of all things. Neither makes central the need for a reference point beyond individual or group expressions of ego. Both are therefore selfish in their own ways – capitalism, on behalf of the individual, and communism, for the group. To see beyond that – beyond self-interested constructs of *Homo*

Box 3: Jamie Whittle
White River: a journey up and down the River Findhorn

My Research

The purpose of the research was to study the human ecology of the River Findhorn; to travel on foot and by canoe the length of the river from coast to mountains and back again; to uncover the rhythms of the river and to attempt to write about the river in a creative way; to extend my own personal parameters by exploring more fully the watershed in which I live, and to strengthen my sense of place; to connect to something larger and older; to blend science with poetry, philosophy with law, and economics with psychology through grounded, integrated study.

My Findings

The River Findhorn is a wild river. It rises in the Monadhliath Mountains to the north of the Cairngorms, runs through the valley of Strathdearn, cuts across the northern fringe of the Dava Moor, then enters a lengthy gorge section that penetrates the forests all the way down to the coastal plain, entering the sea at the Moray Firth. Travelling the river you discover both the diversity and the continuity of a watershed.

Scenically the river is quite stunning, and there can be few rivers throughout the country that compare to its beauty. Yet there are areas where the river and the surrounding land have been abused and where there is major need of restoration. Salmon numbers have declined significantly since the 1960s, vast areas of native forest have been removed in the past three centuries, the last

Box 3: Jamie Whittle *(continued)*

wolf in Scotland was killed near the river in 1743, and remote, rural communities face pressures from a lack of employment and community resources as well as a lack of support from central government to promote and protect the values of this bioregion.

The journey – physical, intellectual, spiritual – affirmed in me the preciousness and aliveness of wild places like the River Findhorn. If we concentrate on building natural capital through habitat and species restoration, so too can we create a much stronger economic platform from which communities can gain stability.

Becoming aware of the place in which you dwell (including the wider watershed) provides a far deeper sense of cultural identity. If spirituality at its most pared down is the practice of tapping into a larger identity whilst participating in the aliveness of the world and witnessing its intricacies and idiosyncrasies, a journey along the length of a river provides an opportunity to move within all these dimensions.

Next Steps

The dissertation was extended into a book entitled *White River* and published by Sandstone Press in Dingwall, Ross-shire in December 2007. The book is now in its second print. Royalties from the book are being committed to ecological conservation work and environmental education along the River Findhorn.

economicus, whether individually or collectively expressed – requires an eye for the deeper dynamics of life. That is where the come-to-pass of our times points to the need also to take spiritual bearings.

Human Ecology of Becoming Existence

During the late 1980s, after my second stint in PNG, I came back home and worked for five years as business advisor to the Iona Community. There I saw people, many of them clergy, wrestling with the human cost of the havoc that "no such thing as society" was wreaking on entire communities of the relatively poor. And after that, from 1990 onwards, I started teaching human ecology, initially at Edinburgh University.

Scholars can spend a lot of time debating what human ecology is. Some say it's the study of PRET or PRED – the interactions of population, resources, environment and either technology or development – both amounting to much the same thing. Others say that human ecology studies interactions between the social environment and the natural environment. Both of these definitions are valid. But more than anything, ecology on its own is simply the study of plant and animal *communities.* This implies that *human* ecology studies *human communities.* And you can't just talk abstractly about that, any more than a fish can get by just gurgling on water! Human ecology has got to be something that you immerse yourself in, living and practising it as well as studying it.

Many academics gurgle aplenty but find this difficult to grasp. The challenges of real-life engagement often seem to trouble their presumption of objectivity. Like my adversary on the Beast of the East, the nature of community is neither obvious nor necessarily desirable. As such, I have noticed that academics often dismiss community as backward and reactionary. On one occasion I rumbustiously debated this in public with Charles Leadbeater, a guru to Tony Blair who had written a book advocating the virtual virtues of the 'knowledge economy'. Fittingly called *Living on Thin Air,* it expressed the view that: "Strong communities can be pockets of intolerance and prejudice. Settled, stable communities are the enemies of innovation, talent, creativity, diversity and . . . the enemy of knowledge creation, which is the wellspring of economic growth."

Box 4: From Papua New Guinea's *Liklik Buk*

- The idea of 'using' the land in the Western sense, the thought of wearing it out, never occurred to the traditional Melanesian community which was 'Alive in the land'.

- PEOPLE are not the problem.
  PEOPLE are what it's all about.
  PEOPLE are the answer.

- Working for the people.
  Working for thank you.
  These are two different things,
  and there is often goal conflict between them.

- Our objective is not to be 'well-liked', but to support people in their processes of growth, whether they like it at the moment or not. In the short run many persons would rather be dependent than alive and growing. So we can't just do whatever people say they want us to do. In the long run, persons appreciate the ones who help them to grow, not the ones upon whom they have become dependent.

All that can sometimes be true, but the alternative – lack of community – can be worse. It's like the old adage, "If you don't like education, try ignorance." In universities and government agencies community is paid lip service. But with scintillating exceptions there is usually a deficit of applied engagement. 'Community' in public discourse too often becomes a synonym for mere consultation or, at best, minimal efforts at participation. Such superficiality is characteristic of the postmodern intellect and social policy. As the cultural historian John Lorne Campbell put it in 1933 when speaking about the Hebridean psyche (but the same could equally apply to many other indigenous peoples):

> The consciousness of the Gaelic mind may be described as possessing historical continuity and religious sense; it may be said to exist in a vertical plane. The consciousness of the modern Western mind, on the other hand, may be said to exist in a horizontal plane, possessing breadth and extent, dominated by a scientific materialism and a concern with purely contemporary happenings. There is a profound difference between the two mental attitudes, which represent the different spirits of different ages, and are very much in conflict.[8]

It is not just ignorance or colonising opportunism that drives this flattening out of the social space-time continuum. It is also fear. When we are inwardly damaged or our personal growth is undeveloped, it is tempting to curl up and hide who, and from who, we really are. We offer to the outer world only the hard edge of an armoured ego. If enough of us do the same, it becomes a social norm.

I think that Fritz Schumacher saw all this. It was why he wrote his chapter on *Buddhist Economics*. To create an "economics as if people mattered," he said, we must learn "to overcome egocentredness by joining with other people in a common task; and to bring forth the goods and services needed for a becoming existence." (4:52)

A "becoming existence"! Let that be our objective. And let us now press deeper into Schumacher's objective to inquire what such an existence might mean. We will start with his diagnosis of what's wrong in the human condition.

Chapter 2

Metaphysical Disease

Many Logs to Make a Blaze

Once when my son Adam was about 10 years old, we went together to a music festival on the remote Scoraig peninsula in the north-west Scottish highlands. Folks from the lowland cities were camped out all over the grassy meadow overlooking Loch Broom. As I walked about, a youth in his mid-teens came running over. His demeanour was typical of a young man from a disadvantaged urban background. "Is that your son?" he asked me, pointing to Adam who, I could see, was sitting with the youth's friends around a fire. "Man . . . he's amazing!"

All that had happened was that Adam had encountered the lads vainly trying to get their campfire going. They'd been holding a cigarette lighter to a single huge log hoping it would eventually ignite! He'd simply shown them how to split it and make some kindling. That way the fire could start small and develop a heart for itself. By stacking larger sticks around in a pyramid, a chimney effect is created that sucks air in and through from underneath. The fire thereby breathes. Bigger sticks catch on from the heat kindled in smaller ones. It takes many logs to make a blaze.

It's the same with the kindling of community. Here, too, the name of the game is creating a heart around a hearth fuelled by many shapes and sizes. These warm and fire one another up. And once again, the right structure is needed at the centre to let fresh air in so that all can breathe. There's one difference between a community and a cult: a community has semi-permeable boundaries that allows for the in and the out of the breath, but in a cult people are trapped, sucked dry and suffocate.

Too many very dry logs will blaze up, burn what's all around about, and burn out in the fire of their own ungrounded enthusiasm that exceeds ability to deliver in a sustained manner. Equally, an unseasoned log placed in the heart of things when still too green and wet is a damper, and can even put the whole fire out.

Our metaphor could be extended endlessly. The essence is that community is about creating synergies out of diverse parts. Just as a skilled fire-keeper has a feel for the qualities of different kinds of wood at different stages of seasoning, so we too must cultivate our understanding of what human beings are if we are to become keepers of community. That is why becoming grounded means having one foot in the physical realities of this world and the other in the dynamics of people.

On the one hand we need to understand *physics* – the properties of matter – as with our practical example of fire-making. That's the realm of things like land, buildings, and knowing the nitty-gritty practicalities of how things work or grow. On the other hand, we must reach behind such outer hardware and get to the software that is the inner nature of being human. Such is the continuum between the *physical* and what philosophers call the *metaphysical*.

The etymology or word-origin of this Greek term is *meta,* meaning beyond, behind or transformed, and *physika,* meaning the nature of physical things or matter. Metaphysics is therefore concerned with what underlies the outer surface of the material world. It means reaching behind the ordinary, using both concept and metaphor to move beyond normal ways of seeing and being, so to discover inner layers of truth that will transform our perception and experience of reality. In the work of community-building, it means reaching behind seeing a human being merely in economic terms – as an entity needing to be fed, clothed and housed – and connecting up such vital practicalities with what it takes to bring a person alive from within. For that life within is the heart of the fire of life. Without it, branches thrown on top will never kindle.

Schumacher talks about metaphysics at least a dozen times in *Small is Beautiful*. We therefore cannot engage adequately with his ideas unless we get metaphysically turned on. This is how he diagnosed the human condition (6:99):

The task of our generation, I have no doubt, is one of metaphysical reconstruction. It is not as if we had to invent anything new; at the same time, it is
not good enough merely to revert to the old formulations. . . . The deepest
problems of our age . . . cannot be solved by organisation, administration, or
the expenditure of money, even though the importance of all these is not
denied. We are suffering from a metaphysical disease, and the cure must therefore be metaphysical.

Why, then, do we not hear more about metaphysics? Why is it not at
the heart of every curriculum and constitution? The answer is that it
has been deliberately marginalised by materialistic philosophers. It
doesn't fit the secular and mechanistic ideology that strips the sacred
from both people and nature.

To remember what metaphysics is, we need to dig backwards. In
1854 the great but now near-forgotten Scottish philosopher James
Frederick Ferrier published his seminal work, *Institutes of
Metaphysic*. He put it ever so simply. He said: "Metaphysics is the science of real existence."[9]

Both Ferrier and Schumacher (6:94) remind us that Aristotle saw
metaphysics as being divided into *being* and *knowing*. The study of
being – that is to say, what we are – is called *ontology*. The study of
knowing – which is to say, what we think we know and how we know
it, including knowing what we don't know – is called *epistemology*.
Dictionaries credit Ferrier with having first introduced this word into
the English language.

An interest in reality thereby places before us the two bottom-line
questions of all philosophy. One is ontological, and the other episte-
mological. 'What are we?' and 'How do we know?' Such is the terri-
tory we must now tread in deepening the question, 'What is
community?'

Essentialism versus Nihilism

Most philosophers who denigrate metaphysics do so out of a distaste,
even a loathing, of *essentialism*. Aristotle had said that the *essence* is
'the substantial reality' of any thing. It is that which 'cannot be
reduced to another definition which is fuller in expression.'[10] It follows
that to be an essentialist is to believe that things really have an existence that is in some way *meaningful*. But to call something essential-

Box 5: Chris Adams
Helping 'Fight or Flight' Take Wing: for Colin Macleod of the GalGael Trust

Autumn 2004 and a storm raged outside. Shadows cast by the fire of our ideas lit and then darkened and then lit again as Alastair tended the hearth. A group of students had gathered to discuss the possibility of embarking on thesis research under Alastair's supervision. Alastair mentioned that he was affiliated with a group of folks in Govan called the GalGael Trust. They had a workshop where they built traditional boats and made things of beauty out of natural materials. There was an opportunity for a couple of students to do some work with them. That was how my time with the GalGael began.

Intending to gather accounts from people within the GalGael community about the 'spirituality of addiction,' I became a regular volunteer. I helped with whatever needed doing and tried not to get in the way. Working side by side with Colin, Tam, Ian, Gehan, Livvy and others, I learned about the deeply purposeful spirit that permeates the GalGael and how it touches the participants on the 'Navigate the Future' program. I also learned about how very badly I needed that same healing. I was not recovering from heroin addiction, I had never been jobless when I did not want to be, I had never seen the inside of a working prison: but there I was bathed, nurtured in the hospitality of a truly 'real' people whose daily actions were peppered with feats of heroism. I was inspired, moved by their living example of regeneration spirituality.

Christmas came and I went home to Canada. Walking amongst the big trees, sea crashing against rock places of my childhood, I began to question what I was doing. Although I had originally signed up to do the CHE MSc over two years, unforeseen administrative factors now meant that I had only one year to complete the course. Already, I was feeling uneasy about forcing the rich modules and thesis into such a short period of time. But my early encounters with the GalGael drove this unease home. Colin Macleod (pictured below), the GalGael's founder, had a profound impact on me: someone whose very life cut through bullshit like a claymore. Leading by action, he shone light upon the 'real'. I decided to go part-time at CHE and complete only the Post-Graduate Certificate. With this decision made, I felt free to explore and enjoy my time in Scotland, nay, on this earth.

I began my time with the GalGael wearing an academic's hat – looking to interpret other people's words. Quickly, though, I came to see that the words of the people with whom I heaved heavy logs and lifted boats needed no interpretation. They spoke for themselves. I saw a new role for myself: helping to bring the natural and active poetry of the GalGael to a wider audience. Eventually, with the help of a local publisher and the generous support of the WWF through funds made available to the CHE, we began to put together a booklet of poems, stories and songs by trainees, employees and people from the larger GalGael community. The pieces that we collected ranged from gritty poems about 'smack' to diary entries about the nurturing and eventual rehabilitation of a house martin by the trainees. I am conscious that the stories that we collected represent only a drop in the ocean of living poetry that resides in the GalGael community but they are a great testament.

Colin's death, just as the booklet was nearing completion, temporarily halted its publication. However, in June 2006, at the celebratory Eagle Night held in Colin's honour, 'Fight or Flight' was launched as Issue 10 of *daemon* from Survivor's Press. I now live in Bristol but I carry with me the lessons that I learned during my time with the GalGael. Whether I am weaving a willow basket, having dinner with my soon-to-be wife or teaching kids about organic agriculture, Colin's active wisdom, the Gael's song is with me always.

ist has become the fashionable academic put-down. Postmodern thought seeks to 'deconstruct', or dismantle, all sense of story and meaning. As Jean-François Lyotard stated it, "I define *postmodern* as incredulity toward metanarratives" – a metanarrative being a 'legitimizing myth' or 'narrative archetype'.[11] Such a mindset views essentialism as an arbitrary mind game of social construction, usually for the self-seeking justification of power. It can of course be that, but it doesn't have to be.

Pressing deeper, I think that the core issue is that essentialism clashes with the mainstream (post)modernist view that only 'positive' materiality – only that which can be proven to exist in physical terms – is real. As such, the body is considered real, but the soul is not. For both modernism and postmodernism – and in my opinion, the one is just an extension of the other – there is no 'beyond' for the metaphysician to get 'behind'! There is no essence, vital presence or spiritual underpinning that underpins the turning of the world.

For example, the fêted philosopher of British logical positivism, Sir Freddie Ayer, said that metaphysics is "literally senseless" because it deals with things that cannot be known through the senses.[12] Such theorists say that our universe is wholly mechanistic. We are biological machines, designed merely for the biochemical replication of what Richard Dawkins called our "selfish genes". There is no essence, whether human or divine. If this is true, then life has no ultimate meaning. Nothing has a point. This philosophy is known as *nihilism*. It canonises the emptiness of nothing.

A good example can be found in the last few lines before the conclusion of *Being and Nothingness*, the seminal work of French existentialist philosopher Jean-Paul Sartre. His bottom line is that "the idea of God is contradictory" and, uttered in the same breath, "Man is a useless passion."[13] He says that it is pointless to get worked up about humanity because emptiness lies at its heart.

For Sartre, we seek meaning in the life around us to dodge the existential angst of our loneliness, but such escapism is what he calls "bad faith". The idea of altruism – what he calls "Being-for-others" – is delusory. Reality is nothing but the solipsism – the lack of relationship with others – of our own private hollow existence. For him, freedom is defined as the 'reflection-reflecting' of our own solitary existences in a hall of mirrors. And what do we see in that reflection of ourselves? We see, he tells us, "the nothingness which is at the heart of man".[14] To look for anything more than that would be, if I might put words into his mouth, nothing but the parched croaking of a thirsty traveller reaching for a mirage.

From such a standpoint there can be no deep basis for community and neither, for that matter, the possibly inconvenient call to responsibility that would accompany it. We see this expressed with a most disturbing clarity in Sartre's views about women. It is not just God and 'Man', he tells us, that are false passions. Equally, a man's search for love with a woman is pointless. We may seek such union with one another, but in his view:

> The obscenity of the feminine sex is that of everything which 'gapes open'. It is an appeal to being as all holes are.... Woman senses her condition as an appeal precisely because she is 'in the form of a hole'.[15]

For a man to venture in to that 'hole' means psychological castration. Sartre continues: "Beyond any doubt her sex is a mouth and a voracious mouth which devours the penis"! Her child is but that which "stops up the hole". At best, "human reality," he goes on to say, can but sit life out alone in the self-referential cave of "its own foundation". Such is the brute reality of our existence. It's like the person who is asked how he is and replies, "just existing". From this bleak outlook existentialism derives its name. As if to avoid any doubt, Sartre famously sums up the bottom line in his 1944 play, No Exit. "Hell is other people."

Of course, there are times when that can be very true! But for the most part, such egotistic chauvinism is surely hard to fathom. Perhaps it is significant that Being and Nothingness was first published in 1943 at the height of the Nazi occupation of France. Others see significance in the fact that Sartre lost his father at a tender age. And yet, in spite of, or perhaps, because of, his nihilism, Sartre continues to be celebrated as one of the greatest philosophers of the 20th century. He was offered but declined a Nobel Prize for literature. Some 20,000 people attended his Paris funeral in 1980. He won acclaim for speaking out about human rights and also during the French student uprising of May 1968 – though it is puzzling how such apparent concern for others squared with his overall philosophy. But at the end of the day, the tragedy of Sartre was that while he could at times brilliantly attack domination

Box 6: *GalGael poetry from 'Fight or Flight'*

from *The Bright Ones*
by Colin Macleod

Listen to the Earth and ancient bard
See the future past and present
Soar on currents no eye can see
Set out on the task of healing
A dying, dying island home . . .
Freedom is here at last

Shug Hamilton carves a Celtic Cross at the GalGael Trust

from *Out of the Darkness*
by George Burton

Out of the darkness. . .
There comes a time when you realise
That you are searching for answers
Then clarity burns in your heart
But I believe in miracles
I believe in something pure
I believe with faith in mind
Nothing can harm you any more

systems, he offered but cold comfort in their place. The fact that he remains a cornerstone of secular humanism is itself a sign of our times.

And Sartre is just one example of the genre of thought that led Fritz Schumacher to conclude that the disease of our times is metaphysical. Another would be Descartes. He nailed dogs by their paws to a board, splayed out for vivisection, telling his observers to ignore their whimpering because these were just the mechanistic creaking of an unoiled machine. Such can be the outcome when soul is denied.

Small is Beautiful uses as an example Bertrand Russell's view (from his essay, 'A Free Man's Worship', 1929) that the whole universe is "the outcome of accidental collocations of atoms" (6:85). This led Russell to the nihilistic conclusion that, "only on the firm foundation of unyielding despair can the soul's habitation henceforth be safely built". For Schumacher there was a direct link between such secular humanism, existential or otherwise, and the mechanistic mindset of contemporary economics. He says (6:84; 7:114):

> Estrangement breeds loneliness and despair, the 'encounter with nothingness', cynicism, empty gestures of defiance, as we can see in the greater part of existentialist philosophy and general literature today. . . . Nature, it has been said, abhors a vacuum, and when the available 'spiritual space' is not filled by some higher motivation, then it will necessarily be filled by something lower – by the small, mean, calculating attitude to life which is rationalised in the economic calculus. . .

What, then, is the alternative to such "a bad, vicious, life-destroying type of metaphysics" (6:89)? It offers only "the triumphant idea of positivism, that valid knowledge can be attained only through the methods of the natural sciences . . . and denies the possibility of objective knowledge about meaning and purpose of any kind" (6:86-7). How, he asks, can we rise beyond such a tone-deaf worldview?

The answer requires that we overcome "the lack of depth" that comes from "the absence of metaphysical awareness" (6:91). Schumacher suggests that "education cannot help us as long as it accords no place to metaphysics" (6:91). To transcend "the idolatry of economism" (7:112), "the idolatry of *enrichissez-vous*, which celebrates millionaires as its culture heroes" (17:248), we are left with no alternative. We must bite the bullet and re-engage with "the most vital ideas about the *inner* development of man" (6:85).

Only by educating for 'whole men' can the 'truly educated man' emerge. Men – and, of course, women equally – must learn to relate to the world not just through the five outer senses, but also, and most crucially he says, by being "truly in touch with the centre" (6:92-3).

That 'centre' is precisely the vitality or essence of life that materialistic philosophies deny. For what is the 'essence', but the interiority or *spirituality* of things.

Now we can see why essentialism has become such a controversial notion! The real issue is not that the Nazis or more recent political parties of the far right have abused it as they have everything else in advancing injurious forms of nationalism. The real issue is that essentialism is philosopher-talk for spirituality. It implicitly challenges us all with the age-old question: "To what do we give our lives?" What is most meaningful to us? In what do we bestow our sense of *worth*?

'Worth' is the Old English root of the word *worship*. As such, our question thereby firms up in a way that disturbingly puts the materialistic mindset on the spot. It becomes the age-old issue of idolatry: *What god do you worship?*

If our 'god' is xenophobic, violent, totalitarian – or, for that matter, mindnumbingly mechanistic – then we will end up replaying the brutality of a Descartes, Stalin, Mao or Pol Pot. Here secularism sets up its idols and then makes out that spirituality doesn't exist, so that it can get away with it. But if, on the other hand, our god is, say, life as love made manifest, then a very different relationship to reality opens out – albeit one that holds us to account.

That is what is so taxing about the metaphysics of essentialism. It forces people to face up to and own their *values*. And spiritually speaking, values are not something that we just invent. They're not the personal or social constructions that secular humanism and its various offshoots try to pass them off as being. True values are a discovery. They're the gift of revelation. They're inner qualities that emerge only as we live up to becoming increasingly honest to life.

As Evelyn Underhill put it in her classic study, *Mysticism*, we are talking here about "the essence of Reality . . . fed from within rather than upheld from without". It manifests, she reminds us, "*Cor ad cor loquitur*" – "heart speaking to heart".[16] And the heart doesn't connect by proudly burnishing and trumpeting its own perfection. That leads only to the conceit of spiritual materialism – the fetishisation of the spiritual path that notches up such performance indicators as church attendance, yoga postures or counting its own generosity. The heart connects by a quality of open honesty. For I do not believe that we can just choose to love as if so doing were an act of will. But we can make the effort to be honest in our relationships – a psychological honesty, which goes much deeper than ordinary truth-telling. This reaches to the truth that sets us free. Then it becomes possible for life's deep grace to thaw the frozen crust around the heart and for the doors of love to open.

Honest-to-life opening of the heart, then, is the metaphysical antidote to nihilism. This, too, is the spiritual grounding of a heart-to-heart cosmology that finds expression in the practice of community; and that as 'communion'.

Such transformative power – radical honesty opening the way to radical grace – is the deepest foundation of empowerment.[17] It transforms other people from being 'holes', or 'Hell', to living logs in the fire of love. As a crazy prophet once put it, "I have come to set fire to the earth, and how I wish it were already kindled!"[18]

Pressing on the G-spot

Here, then, is the Great Work of our times: to know and to strengthen existence as spiritual interconnection. In his *Institutes of Metaphysics,* J. F. Ferrier called it "the theistic conclusion". This refutes the idea that 'Man' is the measure of all things, and puts 'God' – the Tao, Buddha nature, Allah, Brahman, Goddess, Christ, Great Spirit, or whatever we want to call the essential ground of Being – back at the heart of reality.

"Here," said Ferrier, "philosophy has accomplished her final work." Here we discover 'the basis of all religion'. For at the heart of Being, he says, we find not emptiness, but "the One Absolute Existence . . . a supreme, and infinite, and everlasting Mind *in synthesis with all things.*"[19] In other words, a mind illuminated by Spirit.

Such cosmic interplay with the divine is, according to Ferrier, the nature of our essence. I find it remarkable that he was expressing these ideas before Eastern thought had significantly come to the attention of Western intellectuals. This spiritual courage – his home-sprung *jñâna* or intellectual yoga as it would be called in the East – was why he never won the coveted chair in moral philosophy at Edinburgh

Box 7: Brian Thom McQuade
The Cycle of Regeneration: a study of urban community in Govan

My Research

In June of 2006, I was asked by the Centre of Human Ecology to explore the evidence for an elemental connection with place in Govan. I wanted to investigate whether this can help build deeper community of place and thereby form a key element of community cohesion and regeneration in Greater Govan. Put another way, could there be an elemental consciousness lying at the core of the psyche or 'soul' of a community like Govan which can be drawn upon as a resource for the regeneration of an area that has fallen on hard times?

My Findings

I have lived most of my life in Govan and I am involved directly as a volunteer worker with four Govan charities and indirectly with a number of others whose aims are tied in with the regeneration of Govan. My research approach was to interview the staff, volunteers and helpers of these organisations. I used no questionnaires but simply talked to people and let them tell me about their lives, how they became involved with issues of regeneration, why it led them to Govan, why they felt that what they were doing there was important to them, and finally, what their hopes for the future were. Through this method of investigation I found that people 'bared their soul'.

Almost all of the 59 people I spoke to told me that they became involved with community groups because they felt that they didn't 'fit in' elsewhere or that

Box 7: Brian Thom McQuade *(continued)*

they were misunderstood and ultimately, were disappointed by or let down by society at large. Most of them also felt 'driven' to join the organisations that they did because they felt that there, they could do something really worth-while – for themselves and for the communities they served.

I also found that after some time spent in these groups, my interviewees felt that there was a general feeling, almost an obligation, to give something back to the wider community – even though about three-quarters of the people I interviewed did not come from Govan originally. When I asked a number of them why they felt obliged to do so, most replied with the statement, "Well, you just have to, don't you?" I think that this driving force is the elemental spirit of Govan where people who have found something worthwhile in their lives wish to share it with others. My research suggests this to be a 'Cycle of Regeneration' taking place in Govan right now.

Next Steps

I have been down to the Oxfam headquarters in Oxford to present my findings. I continue to be involved in Sunny Govan Radio, the GalGael Trust and other community groups in Govan.

[Brian is pictured here undertaking his pioneering research on early photo-graphic plates, published in monograph as Brian Thom McQuade, *Sir John Lavery and his use of Photography at the Glasgow International Exhibition of 1888*, TH.A.H.M. van Asperen – The Glasgow Art Club, Glasgow, 2006, ISBN 978 0 9552290 08.]

University. As an admirer of the ancient 'pagan' philosophers, he fell into the cleft stick of his times – caught in a crux between, on the one hand, the rising forces of secular positivism, and on the other, the backlash that they provoked in evangelical Christians.

Amongst other things, the evangelicals confused Ferrier's subtle panentheism with pantheism. *Panentheism* understands the divine as being both immanent *and* transcendent, thus 'God in nature', yet not limited to it. But *pantheism*, at least in its more simplistic representations, sees the divine as entirely immanent to this world, thus having a more restrictive perspective of 'God as nature'. As such, the evangelicals' attack was a misplaced caricature of Ferrier's thought. By all accounts he found it painful to the epistemic nether regions; instructively so, for he has not been alone in suffering such a plight. As the humorist of the time, W. E. Aytoun, put it in giving versified voice to the assailants of the Ferrier camp: "We'll call them dull and ignorant, / We'll swear their books are mystical, / And if we find that that won't do, / We'll call them pantheistical."[20]

Ferrier insisted that his essentialism was wholly organic: "a natural growth of old Scotland's soil [that was] born and bred in the country and is essentially native to the soil."[21] But from that soil grew a universal message; one that is germane to any deep understanding of empowerment. That message is that without the faculty of self-consciousness humanity can attain and sustain neither identity (ontology) nor intelligence (epistemology). He says:

> Self-consciousness, therefore, is the essence of the mind, because it is in virtue of self-consciousness that the mind is the mind – that a man is himself. Deprive him of this characteristic, this fundamental attribute, and he ceases to be an intelligence. He loses his essence. Restore this, and his intelligent character returns.[22]

The rebuke to nihilistic philosophers who deny the significance of consciousness is plain. In so doing they also deny humanity the ontological grounding of intelligence. For as Ferrier saw it, self-consciousness arises *in synthesis* between all things and God. John Lennon would partly get the point in a 1970 song that had the lyrics, "God is a concept / by which we measure / our pain." But more than that, God cannot be confined to just a concept. And from this reference point of Grand Cosmic Central Station much more than just pain falls into sharp relief. So too does our joy, love, beauty and all other 'being-val-ues' or 'metavalues' – those that can only be described in terms of sim-ilar values; ones that bridge the immanent and the transcendent.[23] As the American cultural critic George Steiner reminds us in seeing the essentialism of 'real presence' at the heart of beauty: "All good art and literature begin in immanence. But they do not stop there."[24]

Metaphysics therefore matters, and yet in today's world it has been rendered embarrassing. Our grandparents' generation could talk openly about God, but not about 'it' – sex. We've swapped things round. And that's something that needs sorting out, because we're los-ing out on the reality that we can have both.

I therefore mischievously refer to the new 'it' as *pressing on the G-spot* – the God-spot. The parallels are precise. Some people insist the G-spot doesn't exist. Others – often the victims of childhood spiritual abuse – respond with understandable cries of pain. But potentially, the G-spot is just pure ecstasy. In one cultural context it might yield cries of "Jeeesusss!" In another, "Ahhh, Alllahhhhh!"

I could offer more examples, but I'd better not get carried away: the last time I did so – it was while addressing a conference in Ireland – I had a 69-year-old grandmother come up afterwards. "I can assure you," she said, "that it exists. And what's more – it still works!"

All these 'masks of God' are faces of the *philosophia perennis* – the perennial or eternal philosophy. Here differing tributaries of faith all flow down to the same Ocean of Being. This is not about sexual love in just the narrow physical sense. This is the full cosmic mystical mar-riage of the Bible's *Song of Solomon,* or the Sufi hymns of Islam, or Hindu Tantra, or paeans to the Goddess. It is a love that incorporates everything, including all the tenderness and exhilaration of human sexuality.

Fritz Schumacher was unabashed in his willingness to press on the spiritual G-spot. "Strange to say," he tells us, "the Sermon on the Mount gives pretty precise instructions on how to construct an out-look that could lead to an Economics of Survival."

It was also while exploring Jesus' words "Blessed are the peace-makers," that he made the first of only two mentions of his book's famous title: "We need a gentle approach, a non-violent spirit, and small is beautiful" (10:152).

And Schumacher was explicit that Buddhism was only a flag of

convenience for his spiritual version of economics. His position was
fully interfaith (3:50):

> We shall explore what economic laws and what definitions of the concepts 'eco-
> nomic' and 'uneconomic' result, when the meta-economic basis of Western
> materialism is abandoned and the teaching of Buddhism is put in its place. The
> choice of Buddhism for this purpose is purely incidental: the teachings of
> Christianity, Islam, or Judaism could have been used just as well as those of any
> other of the great Eastern traditions.

"There is a revolutionary saying," he also reminds us, that "Man shall
not live by bread alone but by every word of God." And he presses the
G-spot's implications of this all the way home to the mundane world,
fully connecting the immanent with the transcendent (2:30-1):

> The hope that . . . without bothering our heads about spiritual and moral ques-
> tions, we could establish peace on earth, is an unrealistic, unscientific, and irra-
> tional hope. The exclusion of wisdom from economics, science, and technology
> was something which we could perhaps get away with for a little while, as long
> as we were relatively unsuccessful; but now that we have become very success-
> ful, the problem of spiritual and moral truth moves into the central position.
> From an economic point of view, the central concept of wisdom is permanence.
> We must study the economics of permanence.

Triune Basis of Community

Like ecology, economics is a word that derives from the Latin,
oeconomia and the Greek, *oikonomia* – both of which mean 'household management'. For Schumacher, the household in question is the
whole Earth.

The word 'community' derives from the Latin *communitas*. It
means 'fellowship of relations or feelings'. As such, a full understanding of economics – one that doesn't dismiss impacts on the poor or
nature as 'externalities' to the economic equation – must serve the
planetary household in the fullness of its community.

In my view – and I think this is something that I soaked in from the
Hebridean villages where I grew up – such full community has three
pillars. I call them the *triune basis of community*.

Triune means three-in-one. The branches from the vine of life are
separate, yet they derive from a common taproot. Like foliated Celtic

Human Ecology as Full Human Community

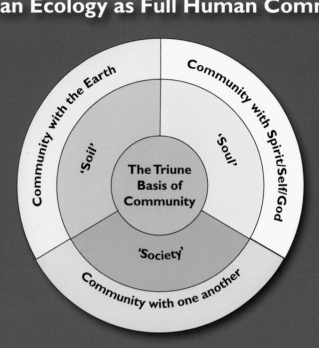

Community with the Earth

Community with Spirit/Self/God

'Soil'

'Soul'

The Triune Basis of Community

'Society'

Community with one another

The Head, Heart & Hand of Engagement

Head
(reason, logic, law ... *enforcement*)

Heart
(feelings, intuition, values ... *processes*)

Hand
(management, serving, activism ... *enabling*)

Simplified Structure of the Human Psyche
(based on C. G. Jung)

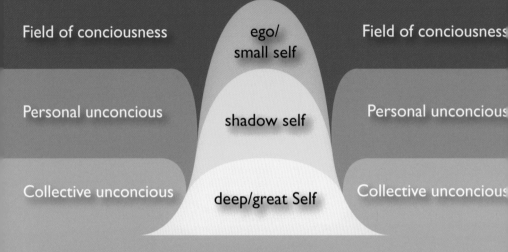

Field of conciousness   ego/ small self   Field of conciousness

Personal unconcious   shadow self   Personal unconcious

Collective unconcious   deep/great Self   Collective unconcious

The Transpersonal Basis of Community
After Jolande Jacobi, 1942

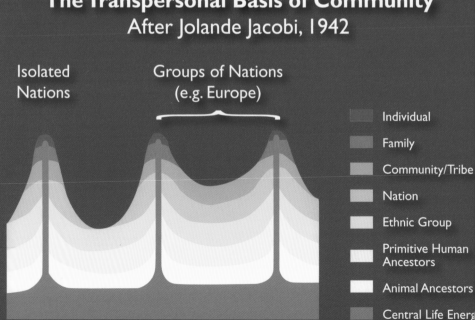

Isolated Nations

Groups of Nations (e.g. Europe)

Individual

Family

Community/Tribe

Nation

Ethnic Group

Primitive Human Ancestors

Animal Ancestors

Central Life Energ

The Cycle of Belonging

4. Sense of
Responsibility
(action - 'hand')

1. Sense of
Place
(grounding)

Place
=
nature
+
culture

3. Sense of
Values
(soul - 'heart')

2. Sense of
Identity
(ego - 'head')

The Rubric of Regeneration

Re-membering ...
that which has been dismembered

Re-visioning ...
how the future could be

Re-claiming ...
what is needed to bring it about

Community
Regeneration

Walter Wink's Trilogy of Empowerment

Naming the Powers

Unmasking the Powers

Engaging the Powers

The Powers that Be

The Wheel of Fundamental Human Needs

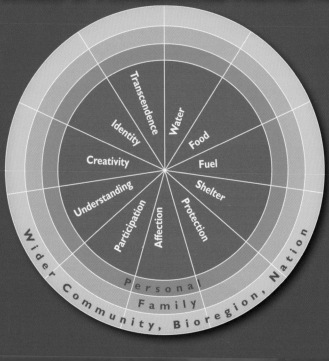

Transcendence

Identity

Water

Food

Creativity

Fuel

Understanding

Shelter

Participation

Protection

Affection

Personal

Family

Wider Community, Bioregion, Nation

knotwork, they intertwine. To name them separately is therefore only
a method of conceptualisation. These three branches, or pillars, are:

> *Community with nature;*
> *Community with the divine, and;*
> *Community with one another.*

Because they interlace, constantly melding into one anther, the ordering is not important. I have laid them out as I have here because, when
I discussed it with Satish Kumar of Schumacher College in England,
he told me: "Yes – that is precisely what I describe as *soil, soul and
society*." That alliteration wonderfully sums it up. I have expressed
this ontology of community graphically in the colour *Plate 1* (*Human
Ecology as Full Human Community*).

This triune basis of human ecology or human community can be
glimpsed in teaching and stories from all over the world. For example,
after long preparation the Buddha went and sat under a Banyan tree
('soil'), received enlightenment ('soul'), and then set out to teach community amongst the people ('society').

Consider, too, the temptation of Christ. For me this is a kind of living parable – a spiritual teaching story, and it matters not a jot
whether it is literally true. After all, the gospels themselves manage to
muddle up the ordering of the events. This makes it difficult to argue,
as would some fundamentalists, that the stories of Jesus must be read
literally. Where the soul is concerned, metaphor speaks truth more
loudly than fact. As a priest in the Solomon Islands, John Roughan,
once put it to me, a parable is an armour-piercing missile. It penetrates
the outer defences of ego consciousness and softly explodes its meaning through progressively deeper layers of the human heart. That's the
power of what we're dealing with in this tale.

The story starts shortly after Jesus' baptism at the age of 30. The
Spirit (of God) 'leads' and even, depending on which gospel, 'drives'
him out into the wilderness. The latter is an interesting word. It
reminds us that the spiritual journey is not always chosen. That is why
people talk of having a 'vocation' or 'calling' from beyond their conscious ken. What we see here, then, is the young man, just initiated,
and being taken on his shamanic journey or vision quest.

Once out in the wilds he fasts for '40 days and 40 nights'. We need
to read that metaphorically too. It suggests an encounter with both

Box 8: Sam Harrison
Grounded Philosophy and the Practice of Wisdom

My Research

Through volunteering with the GalGael Trust in Govan, the question of how and why community regeneration had not already 'been so successful so as to put itself out of business' emerged as the focus of my research. The leaders of the Trust were concerned to find out how the GalGael was perceived within the sphere of community regeneration, and what made their approach distinctive. I conducted interviews with key informants in the regeneration policy and service framework of Greater Govan whilst also discussing these topics with members of the GalGael. I hoped to draw conclusions about the origins of the breakdown in Govan's community health, effective methods for its 're-vision', and the possibilities for regenerating community globally.

My Findings

My approach to this research can be called *Grounded Philosophy*. It draws on a Grounded Theory analysis of the experiences of my interviewees in regenerating Govan. Returning to the sense of philosophy as 'love of wisdom', the underlying methods and significance of the GalGael Trust's work became apparent. From this, fundamental conclusions emerged about the wisdom of regeneration policies and practices whilst remaining grounded in concrete experience.

Box 8: Sam Harrison *(continued)*

Conclusions were drawn from interviewee statements relating to a number of different levels:

- Practical issues of community regeneration – the GalGael's delicate balance between business and communitarian principles.
- The globalised economics which triggered the breakdown in this locale, and is often expected to regenerate community, revealing an underlying approach removed from context, feeling or wise action.
- And from this, the role that abstract and dualised thinking has played in the creation of a marginalised community.

In highlighting the harmful results of abstract thought and action, the success of embodied approaches to understanding could be seen in the GalGael's methods. This included the reversal of the separation of 'us' from 'them' thereby preventing the conversion of disadvantaged people into 'commodities' for a 'regeneration industry'. It became clear that the GalGael offers an inspirational model of holistic engagement with current issues. It achieves this through a simple but inclusive traditional skills workshop. Members of this community have a beneficial impact on environmental, psychological and social problems. Through rootedness in people and a place, in hearts and hands, the GalGael Trust's approach is comprehensible and practical.

Next Steps

I am currently running my own business, *Open Ground,* working with communities and businesses to engage deeper with local environmental issues through trips into the hills. I continue to be involved with the GalGael Trust (www.GalGael.org), recently evaluating their *Navigate the Future* training programme (now called *Navigate Life*), and helping develop their 'Rural Vision'. I am also undertaking a PhD in Outdoor Education at the Moray House School of Education, Edinburgh University.

light and darkness – good trip and bad trip.

Jesus is now away from all the chitter-chatter and busyness that normally prevents the inner life from surfacing. He's laid down his carpentry tools, closed the sacred books and turned off the TV. Now he is 'alone' – *all-one* – and gradually he finds himself in the presence, we're told, of wild animals, angelic helpers and of course, Auld Nick himself.[25]

Psychologically the Devil is the 'shadow' side of each one of us; indeed, 'he' is the shadow side of all worldly existence. Mark's gospel calls him 'Satan', but Matthew and Luke use the Greek word *diabolos*, which in turn comes from *diaball*, meaning 'to throw something across.' The usage is well captured by a juggler's *diabolo*. Here two sticks, joined by string, toss a fast-spinning disk dramatically up and down and from side to side.

This points us towards the word's secondary and psychologically more important meaning, which is to throw something across someone's way. It makes them stumble. Greek dictionaries therefore give the derived meaning of *diaball* as being 'to traduce, calumniate, slander, accuse or defame'. All these reveal the 'diabolic' as that underhand dynamic that trips up right relationship. Such is the working through of the lie.

The 'Devil' here emerges as a Jungian archetype – as a pattern, constellation or psychic complex that orders, or rather, disorders the energies of life. And what does this spin-doctor do? He picks up each of the three pillars of community, and one after the other, hurls them across Jesus' path. He tries to trip the young man up. And big time!

In Matthew's ordering of events, the first temptation of Christ is to turn the stones into bread. It seems like rather a quaint enticement, but think about it. It's not just that Jesus himself was peckish after 40 days and nights. It's far bigger than that.

In his novel, *The Brothers Karamazov*, Dostoevsky has the tyrannical cardinal, the Grand Inquisitor, discuss this temptation with Christ, who has been locked up by the Church while attempting his Second Coming. His revolutionary spirituality is a danger to the socially dominating power structures of state-sanctioned religion. The prophet must therefore be kept from the people.

In what is one of the most reprinted passages from any novel, the Inquisitor enters the jail and perversely tries to justify himself. He reminds Christ of the stones on the mountain, and remarks: "Turn them into bread, and mankind will come running after You, a grateful and obedient flock, although they will always tremble in fear that You may withdraw Your hand and stop their supply of bread."[26]

In today's world we could equate this with some of the temptations of industrial agriculture that degrade the soil and inflict animal and human suffering. In a more general sense, we see here the temptation to break community with the Earth. We see *the abuse of nature's power*. But in its vulnerability, nature stands revealed as one pillar of community.

In the second temptation, Christ is taken to a high place – one gospel version has it as the temple, where everybody would have been able to see him and be impressed. He is urged to jump off. The Devil's idea is to prove that God would magically intercede by sending angels to save him. This would show religious clout. But Jesus replies that he will not put God to the test. Here, then, is the temptation to break community with the divine. We see *the abuse of spiritual power*. As such, the divine stands revealed as another pillar of community.

The third temptation is when the Devil offers power over all the kingdoms of the world. This is the temptation of political, military, corporate and proprietary might – the lure of the king, soldier, magnate and landlord. But we should remember the Persian proverb that behind every rich person is a devil; and behind every poor one, are two! The poor must be mindful both of their own devil and that of what they might become if given half a chance! As such, Christ's third temptation, if not actual within us all, is at least latent. It concerns the breaking of community with others – *the abuse of social power*. It reveals the social realm as a pillar of community.

Inner and Outer Work

And there we have it – the triune basis of human ecology as soil, soul and society. The breaking of friendship with any one of these ruptures the fabric of reality. Theologians refer to it with that cringe-inducing little word 'sin'. Schumacher understood this well. It is the root of what he meant by metaphysical disease – a term that he borrowed from R.G. Collingwood, who was professor of metaphysical philosophy at Oxford during the Second World War (6:90).

Buddhist economics, then, is an attempt to heal the ruptures of transgression in the household of the world. It aims, Schumacher tells us, at "producing a high degree of human satisfaction by means of a relatively low rate of consumption." It thereby "allows people to live without great pressure and strain and to fulfil the primary injunction of Buddhist teaching: 'Cease to do evil; try to do good'" (4:56).

As such, a spiritual metaphysics sees "the essence of civilisation not in a multiplication of wants but in the purification of human character" (4:53). And why does purification matter? Because without it, our eyes grow progressively dim to reality. Reality is the Absolute on which all our knowing and being depend. As a mystic up a mountain once said: "Blessed are the pure of heart, for they shall see God."[27]

To cultivate that purity of heart is the work of the inner life that, alone, can hold our outer lives in right relationship. It is why humankind cannot live from bread alone. It is the only way to heal the metaphysical disease that, as I have explored in my book about climate change, *Hell and High Water*, manifests today in threats to the very fabric of this Earth.

Hell, as Dostoevsky tells us, is not other people: "It is the suffering caused by not being able to love any more . . . the flames of thirst for spiritual love."[28] Inner development is the cure for that suffering. Community is its outward flowering. That is why most religions have special names for the spiritual community – the *Ummah* in Islam, the *Noble Sangha* in Buddhism, the *Church* in Christianity.

Schumacher's very last lines in *Small is Beautiful* sum it all up. He says (Epilogue:293):

> Everywhere people ask: 'What can I actually *do*?' The answer is as simple as it is disconcerting: we can, each of us, work to put our own inner house in order. The guidance we need for this work cannot be found in science and technology, the value of which utterly depends on the ends they serve; but it can still be found in the traditional wisdom of mankind.

What we see here, then, is that the inner house, or inner life, is no mere added 'dimension'. Rather, it is the absolute underpinning of the becoming existence. To realise it means deepening ourselves. It is something that we must do both quietly alone and in vibrant community – individually and collectively. I think that such work is helped by having a measure of shared concepts and language. Cultivating psychospiritual literacy is therefore the task towards which we will now turn.

Chapter 3

The Cycle of Belonging

Psychospiritual Literacy

Here I want to present a model of the human psyche and another of how it perhaps functions in community. These relate our individuality to community. We must remember that models always present a simplified, imperfect and contestable view of reality. But at least they offer a starting point, and it is from here that we will seek to clarify a shared language of psychospiritual literacy.

I often use the expression 'psychospiritual' because it allows others the option of looking on these things as being either psychological or spiritual – or both. But really, the Latin word *psyche* derives from the Greek, *psykhe*, which means the soul, mind, spirit, breath, or life. Materialistic ideology has degraded this. Its reductionism has spun the word 'psychology' into a diminished redefinition as *the study of behaviour*. But that is merely behaviourism, cognitive or otherwise. Such behaviourists should own up to their paucity of perspective rather than continue to colonise the etymological energy of a much richer epistemology. I would define colonisation as the presumption of right to take that which has not been given.[29] We should therefore insist on decolonising psychology and restoring its meaning as *the study of the soul*. Meanwhile, and while people think about this, the word 'psychospiritual' provides us with a useful bridging term.

In *Plate 1* we have already seen the triune basis of human ecology expressed as the soil, soul and society of human community. I must ask the reader for the sake of this discussion to let me proceed with that as our core ontology, our shared language of the structure of being. Its corresponding epistemology – its way of knowing reality –

is put forward in the colour *Plate 2* as *Head, Heart and Hand*. At the Centre for Human Ecology we have always made this central to our teaching. The alliteration comes from the work of the Swiss educationalist, Johann Pestalozzi (1746-1827) and the pioneering Scotttish human ecologist, Professor Patrick Geddes (1854-1932).

Geddes ordered the "three H's", as he called them, Heart, Hand and Head. His biographer, Philip Boardman, explains:

> These terms and their sequence simply meant that priority must be given first to the child's emotional development, thereafter to physical growth, and only finally to strictly intellectual training. For him the basis of all elementary education was to be found in childish interests in the natural world and in the wonderment it evoked.[30]

Boardman goes on to quote Geddes, that: "Good teaching begins, neither with knowledge nor discipline, but through delight." It requires developing "the feeling for the subject". We might sum it up that sense leads to essence.

Why have I ordered the three H's differently? My work is about developing what my colleague Sam Harrison and I refer to as a 'grounded philosophy' – one that emerges bottom up from practical experience. Most of the people with whom I work are adults, not children, and prior educational patterns dispose them to starting from the head. The first step to a wider epistemology is to join this up with the emotions and values of the heart.

A good example can be seen in *A Sand County Almanac*, written in 1949 by the great American biologist Aldo Leopold. This classic work of natural ecology advances Leopold's 'land ethic'. He says: "A thing is right when it tends to preserve the integrity, stability, and beauty of the biotic community. It is wrong when it tends otherwise."[31]

More than linking just head and heart, Leopold also points towards the need for practical engagement with the land – the applied domain of the 'hand'. Hand then becomes the ways of knowing that derive from doing. It includes digging and planting the soil, managing conservation programmes, being of service, engaging in activism to care for a place, and enabling others.

The appropriate ordering of head, heart and hand – facts, feelings, actions – therefore depends on context. But ultimately, like with our triune basis of community, the 3-Hs all interweave. Their integration is what signifies a person who has been roundly *educated* as distinct from one who has been merely *instructed*.

If we can, as I might have said in my one-time mechanics class, 'fire on all three cylinders' like this, we are then and only then epistemologically equipped to ask what it really means to be a human being.

Are we just individual egos on legs, driven by selfish genes with no purpose other than self-replication? Is that the shrivelled and shrunken vision of our lot and nihilism, indeed, annihilation, its logical conclusion? Or do realities like Leopold's sense of natural beauty, not to mention the power of love, point beyond this? Are we more than just what appears within the confines of space and time? Is the soul eternal and interconnected in relationships that we might call meaningful?

At this point I must ask my reader to take with me a leap of faith and consider *Plate 3 (Simplified Structure of the Human Psyche)*. This presents a model that can be used to unpack my version of psychospiritual literacy. In this I draw on both mystical and indigenous traditions of the world and, with considerable simplification, on the analytical psychology of the great Swiss psychiatrist, Carl Gustav Jung (1875-1961). I have filtered these through my own experience of what matters most in helping people to understand community dynamics. Let us explore the three levels of being that it portrays.

The Ego and Field of Consciousness

If we think of the fullness of a human being as like an island in the sea, the visible part that protrudes above the water is the ego. *Ego* is simply the Latin for 'I'. It means the conscious 'me' – the Alastair McIntosh who knows himself to be a writer, activist, husband, and so on. Many people associate the word 'ego' with Sigmund Freud, but it was in use well before him. In 1854, two years before Freud's birth, J. F. Ferrier said:

> The words 'ego', 'me', or 'self', have been repeatedly used in the course of these discussions, because, awkward and barbarous though they be, they are of a less hypothetical character than any other terms which can be employed to express what is intended. Whatever else a man may be, he is, at any rate – himself. He understands what he means when he utters the word 'I'.

Ferrier goes on to explain that this 'I' knows itself as an "independent totality" through synthesis of "the singular and the universal".[32] Unlike

Box 9: Rutger Henneman
The Spirituality and Theology of Scotland's Modern Land Reform

My Research

During my studies (two years of forestry, a BSc in history, and now a MSc in 'international development studies' at Wageningen University in the Netherlands) I came to the conclusion that our Western 'modern' patterns of property as applied to land, especially its consequence in 'landlessness' for the major masses of people, is our most pervasive form of oppression. It runs counter to the radical love of Jesus Christ, the Buddha, and the central teaching in the Bhagavad-Gita. I was aware of the potential of Scotland's experience with community-based land reform to redress the issue. With great happiness I took the internship opportunity that Alastair McIntosh offered me: to come and study the role of spirituality and theology in Scotland's modern land reform.

My Provisional Findings

My research comprised a literature review and conducting 15 interviews with 'key land reformers'. These were, first of all, leaders of the successful land reform movements in Assynt, on the Isle of Eigg, and on the Isle of Gigha, and, secondly, theologically informed figures whose thought contributed to the national movement that led to the passing of the Land Reform (Scotland) Act 2003.

Box 9: Rutger Henneman *(continued)*

I found that most of these 15 land reformers challenged the modern 'free market' conception of land as the 'ownership' of a 'commodity'. Most but not all of the land reformers held a personal spiritual position, and the most fierce attacks on landlordism were embedded in theology. These included invoking in a local and present-day context such metaphors or notions as 'Egypt', 'the Promised Land', 'stewardship', 'sin', prophetic warnings against 'joining fields to fields' and 'Jubilee justice' as drawn from Biblical theology. Interviewees commonly made reference to the claim in Psalm 24 that "The Earth is the Lord's, and the fullness thereof."

As well as giving a basis for rejecting the idea of land as absolute private property (Leviticus 25:23), this alternative framework to that of market commodification helped to legitimise the struggle. Although Scotland is largely secular like most other European nations, it was clear that individual leaders and, in some cases, wider reference groups in their communities, drew strength from having a theological underpinning to their arguments. In some cases these also served as a spiritual 'weapon' against the imposing posturing of landed power.

Our data shows how spiritualities might involve 'modes of being' grounded not only in oneself, but in 'the other': in 'nature', in 'community' or in God. Service to the community gives expression to the emergence of an extended sense of identity in solidarity with these. It manifests as a strongly expressed bond of 'belonging' to the land. And finally, many of the respondents saw land reform as a struggle for freedom. It offered them and their communities a lively experienced 'mode of being and becoming free'.

Next Steps

With Alastair McIntosh I am writing an article on this project. At the same time I am finishing my MSc studies by writing two philosophical treatises: an analytical one about power, property and oppression, and an ethical philosophical one to build a spiritual ideology of property and power, based on a spirituality of love understood as selflessness. I am balancing this intellectual work with practice by being involved with the NGO 'de boerengroep' based in the Netherlands. A report on my project is forthcoming as Rutger Henneman, 'Spirituality and Theology in Scotland's Modern Land Reform', *Anthropological Journal of European Cultures* 17(1), 2008.

Sartre's infinite regress of mirrors reflecting back on themselves, this self-knowing is a living relationship between our individuality and the universe. Such is what Jung called the field of consciousness; indeed, expanding consciousness.

To many behavioural scientists, the ego self and its field of consciousness is just a side effect of brain chemistry. As Hans Eysenck of the Institute of Psychiatry personally told me in Aberdeen in 1975: "I consider that consciousness is an epiphenomenon of brain activity."

Here consciousness is at best construed as the beam of a lighthouse atop our island in the sea, sweeping out from the brain-generated ego. But Eastern religions and the spiritual (or 'transpersonal') psychology of people like Carl Jung see it the other way round. For them, cosmic consciousness is the fundamental reality. The brain acts like a tuner or reducing valve that focuses the universal down to the singular. As such, the ego is our individualised share in the transpersonal. To imagine that the brain generates ego consciousness would be as ridiculous as to think that a radio receiver generates the programmes broadcast on the airwaves.

Psychologically speaking, the work of the first half of life is to establish a strong ego identity. This is achieved mainly through work in the outer world. It means learning to keep ourselves clean and fed, getting socialised and educated, making a living, and forming families and other relationships. But it is not sufficient only to remain at this outer level of operating forever. In time, the oil in the lamp of life that was our birthright will run low. We will fall into the danger of burning out or selling out.

A new approach then becomes necessary to see us through the second half of life. To further bolster the ego at this point would only make it brittle. We see this in those perpetual Peter Pans who try to act young when they should be assuming the dignity of age. They have no depth to call upon and so they get stuck in their own narcissistic self-representation. This is the Peak Oil crisis of life. There are fewer and fewer wells to be struck out there. Those who still yearn for new supplies can grab or bomb their way towards more, but it becomes increasingly unseemly. The flame of the lamp of life flickers, and desperately they live off bygone outer achievements, including the power of accumulated money. Indeed, money is very often the last refuge of those who have developed no inner wellhead.

The task of the second half of life is, therefore, to grow psychos-
pirituaIly.[33] This work is variously called self-realisation, self-actuali-
sation and individuation. It means shifting from being self-centred to
becoming a centred self. From now on, the oil that keeps the flame
must come increasingly from within. This was what Schumacher, as
we have seen, called "getting in touch with the centre". Here is the
inner essence, and "Yea, though I walk through the valley of the
shadow of death" the lamp stays bright, and we fear no ill.

The two halves of life focused respectively on the outer and inner
do not necessarily follow chronological age. Most of us move in and
out of both at different times. Some people start second-half-of-life
work in their childhood. Others flounder about like overgrown
teenagers late into their retirement years. Bereft of fitting wisdom, this
is metaphysical disease individually expressed at its most dangerous
and demeaning. As I once heard an old Quaker woman say, "It is per-
ilous to neglect one's spiritual life." We can run from the setting sun
of the ego's slow nemesis, but there is no running away. Sooner or
later the Great Cosmic Conveyor Belt of Life will hit terminus, and
death is but the dissolution of the outer world of the ego self.

And that's the problem with ungrounded egocentricity. If we have
not allowed something more to be made of ourselves, what more can
there be? The only cure, as Schumacher saw so clearly, is metaphysical reconstruction. But that reconstruction implies a sure foundation.
What is it? On what bedrock does this island in the sea repose?

The Deep Self and Collective Unconscious

The elders and elder traditions of the world tell us that the only sure
foundation for metaphysical reconstruction is the ground of being.[34]
We can call it what we want – the divine, or God, will sufficiently
serve my purposes here. It surpasses understanding, so we should be
careful what we say it is or what we think it is not. Even Thomas
Aquinas, the great scholastic theologian who wrote the 'Theory of
Everything' of his times, the commanding *Summa Theologica,* con-
ceded in his dying words on the morning of 6th December 1273: "I
can do no more. Such secrets have been revealed to me that all I have
written now appears of little value."

Jung calls this bedrock of being the Self – usually with a capital S
to distinguish it from the small self of the ego. It is where the inner life

Box 10: Chriss Bull
Women's Identity, Boarding School and Land Ownership

My Research

My study explored the effects of a boarding school education on women's identity and their relationship to the land. Historically the private British boarding school system and the ethos of Empire were symbiotically related. Boarding schools equipped the ruling class to dominate those of 'lower' class or ethnic category.

Using a grounded theory approach, underpinned with an eco-feminist and post-colonial lens, 17 women in Scotland shared their stories. All had attended either private boarding institutions (12, from 'privileged' backgrounds) or state hostels (five, from crofting backgrounds), having been dislocated from their home and land environment usually in pre-adolescence.

My Findings

Most of the women felt that their sense of identity and their psycho-emotional state had been damaged in the process of boarding. Surviving and gaining status within boarding institutions required swift adoption of strategic thinking, strategic relationships and managing one's emotions.

'Attachment theory' stresses a child's need for intimate environmental and emotional security, but boarding environments traditionally often encouraged or even demanded competitive and strategic responses to a 24/7 institutional life. Divide and rule dynamics thereby have the opportunity to flourish. This advances the notion that adolescents 'learn to stand on their own two feet' and that boarding, at least in the private schools, is therefore 'the making of them'. Meanwhile, hearts and minds become trained to detach from authentic feeling and community.

Most women across both social groupings in my sample acknowledged that they found it difficult to trust others and relax into group environments. Most visibly, the upper class women lived physically separate from surrounding communities, buffered by significant land holdings. Furthermore most of the private ex-boarders admitted they felt possessive and territorial in arguably compensatory ways – over their land, space and privacy. This sheds light on dynamics of land ownership that extend beyond usual considerations of economics and status. It touches on a need for control – both physical and emotional – that was out of bounds during adolescence.

In contrast, when the crofters left their state hostels most returned to their crofting roots and, like the upper classes, relished the space that being on their land provided. They, however, went home to close knit communities that relied upon the sharing of resources and energy. Their reason for being boarders was not social grooming, but because their homes were in remote rural areas.

The implication of my findings to the spirituality of community regeneration is extensive. Psycho-emotional wounds that impede emotional maturation cause obstruction to that which gives life and love. The wounds of landed 'privilege' have implications beyond their own household, and may be projected onto tenants on their properties. In the context of Scotland's evolving land reform programme, any critique of landed power thereby inevitably assails the ontology of the landowner. This suggests an imperative of liberation not only for the oppressed, but the real or perceived oppressors as well.

Next Steps

I am living in my homeland *Aotearoa*/New Zealand working with an NGO called *Nga Uruora Kapiti* Project on ecological conservation and restoration along the coast where I live. Undertaking my research re-minded me of my own need to 'return to the land'. NUKP has a strong focus on (re)connecting people to their place through volunteering, social events, political environmental activism and offering places for young offenders to complete 'community service' with us.

The Oral History Society (University of Essex) is to publish a paper on this research – Chriss Bull, Alastair McIntosh and Colin Clark, 'Land, Identity, School: Exploring women's identity with land in Scotland through the experience of boarding school', *Oral History* – due late in 2008.

unites into the life of God. As St Paul put it, "I live, yet not I, but Christ lives within me."³⁵ As Hinduism puts it, Atman (individual self) is Brahman (universal Self) – *tat tvam asi* – "Thou art that."³⁶

These are realms that are not usually conscious to most people. Jung sees the domain of the Self as being in the "collective unconscious" – collective because it is transpersonal, or shared in common with others. In revising some of Jung's ideas, the Italian psychologist Roberto Assagioli suggested that 'super-conscious' might be a better expression.³⁷ But given that it remains beyond the ken of most of us most of the time, I will stick with Jung's nomenclature for present purposes.

To speak or know about the unconscious by definition presents real difficulties. Towards the end of his autobiography, the philosopher Alan Watts describes visiting Jung in 1960. He says it was clear that the old man never intended his concepts to be more than 'heuristic devices' – in other words, speculative trial and error models. In neatly encapsulating the problem of the relationship between the ego and the deeper contents of the unconscious, Watts says towards the end of *In My Own Way*:

> The difficulty [is] that the light of consciousness doesn't illumine its own source; that it is a scanning process, like a thin beam, which can only focus on one small area at a time – and how could we call to memory things we had never noticed unless the unconscious were in some way conscious apart from the scanning beam?

Watts adds that Jung seemed "intensely interested in this, probably because, as I understood, he had rather recently had his own experience of cosmic consciousness transcending the ego . . . which he mentions at the end of *Memories, Dreams, Reflections*."

What such mystical insight reveals is that our small selves, our egos, have always rested upon a much greater foundation in what I call the 'Godspace'. Self-realisation is the awakening to this and starting to live out its implications. This is the work of opening the heart and gradually realising God consciousness. It is both the origin and the deepest end of community – the *Alpha* and the *Omega* of life.

If it all sounds so simple, then what's the problem?

The Shadow Self and Personal Unconscious

The problem is that narrow fringe of storm-tossed rocky water between the island with the lighthouse and its roots deep in the waters of the collective unconscious. Here we have what, to Freud, was the entire *unconscious*, but what Jung saw as being only the *personal unconscious* – that part of the unconscious that is unique to each individual's life experience.

For Freud, this was the basement of the psyche where all in our lives that we have wilfully or unconsciously repressed is dumped. Such contents can moulder for many years. But sooner or later the smell comes up the stairs. It permeates the living room, and guests start to notice. This is the origin of most neurosis and, in the extreme, of psychosis. For Freud, it mainly had to do with repressed issues from childhood sexuality and how our parents related to us.

Jung saw it as much more than just that. He found it helpful to personify psychodynamic patterns and principles as what he called 'archetypes'. An archetype is a recurring major 'complex' or constellation of psychic energy or 'libido'; one that is 'toned' or given its character by powerful forces of myth and emotion. The ego is the main archetypal reality that corresponds to the field of consciousness. Jung called the main archetypal representation which corresponds to the personal unconscious the 'shadow'. In *Plate 3* I have taken the liberty of calling it the 'shadow self' since I want to suggest a tier of three main levels of being – ego self, shadow self and the great Self.

As well as comprising all the things that Freud saw as the repressed contents of the unconscious, Jung additionally recognised the shadow as holding the keys to our unrealised potential. As such, Jungians sometimes say that 90 percent of the shadow is gold dust. It is the coalface of psychospiritual growth. It stands, after all, in the liminal realm – the threshold between ego and God consciousness. That is why, if we want to know God, we must wrestle at one level or another with 'the Devil'. That's what Jesus was doing up the mountain.

Whilst recognising that psychologists dispute the meanings and meaningfulness of all these concepts, I personally would see the shadow as largely comprising the ego's alter ego. The brighter the light of the ego, the longer the shadow it casts. For example, outwardly I am a moderately successful writer who produces books about things like community. That's all very well, but there's a downside. Getting good at what I do has meant, ever since childhood, spending hours at study. These days I'm too often glued to the computer. These activities diminish my engaged connection with others. As such, I may understand a fair bit

Box 11: Iain MacKinnon
Lost Leaders: issues of change and identity in a Highland community

My Research

My focus emerged from a series of conversations with community elders in my home area of Sleat and Strath in the south of Skye. The title (borrowed from Browning's poem on Wordsworth) refers to the infiltration of Highland culture by neighbouring ones that appear to place greater value on material priorities and less on the spiritual.

The research has created a context in which surviving indigenous voices in Sleat and Strath could tell their stories. From these, informed by theoretical work from the social sciences, I have drawn up a case study of how a distinctive way of life was systematically diminished by the values and attitudes of modernity, and the consequences of that process for the carriers of culture – the 'lost leaders'. I now hope to work with the elders in drawing up policy recommendations. These might help to foster a public climate more conducive than previously towards carrying traditional values forward into the future.

My Findings

The importance of this research is both personal and public. I am the non-crofting non-native-Gaelic-speaking son of a Gaelic-speaking crofter. I am seeking to understand the forces that have shaped such a situation. I do not deny the personal, and urgent, nature of my inquiry and, therefore, a substantial element of the project is either overtly or tacitly auto-ethnographic.

Box 11: Iain MacKinnon *(continued)*

In the public sphere there is a well publicised Gaelic renaissance going on in Scotland at the moment. However there appears to be some uncertainty as to what constitutes a Gaelic identity.

Issues of language and place seem to be to the fore in many existing studies. My initial research suggests that, when a Freirian critical consciousness is applied to conversational situations with older Gaels, a more subtle definition of their Gaelic identity emerges.

While, in some senses, Gaelic appears to be reviving the same does not seem to be true of the crofting system of agriculture in which the traditional Gaelic speaking communities have been rooted.

As I undertake the project and connect with my people I can feel nourishment feeding the root system that informs my own sense of who I am. I feel there is a sense in which I am being reclaimed by my own from modernity. The deep comfortable feelings of connection and love that I feel in the presence of these people is an urgent cosmic signal to grow upwards

Next Steps

I am studying for a PhD at the Academy for Irish Cultural Heritages at the University of Ulster, Northern Ireland. This takes further the research that I started for my master's degree with the Centre for Human Ecology at Strathclyde University with support from WWF International.

about community, but I also carry within me an awkwardness about it. There's a personal gaucheness . . . not least because my head often floats off elsewhere when I'm meant to be giving attention. I don't know how much others notice it, but my wife certainly does. Ouch!

The problem is not that we and our organisations have shadow selves. The problem is their denial. That's when the *diabolos* spins into the path and trips people up. I call them 'shadowstrikes' – those unpleasant little interpersonal dynamics that inexplicably come about, setting loose strange moods and bad energy. What we must remember is that a shadow denied is a shadow cast, or projected, onto others. That's why we can often learn most about our own shadow selves by observing what, without clear reason, irritates us most in others. Ouch!

True community in the company of others is always intense because it is the crucible in which psychological 'shit' comes up from the basement. The psyche has a natural impulse to heal. It won't forever suffer its blockages and wounds in festering silence. It will insist on neurotically playing them out to be noticed. Truth will out. Aspiring healthy communities therefore need to understand the psychodynamics of shadow-work. They need to learn how to recognise the shadow and process such symptoms as conflicts and moodiness. That is what makes psychospiritual literacy such an important starting off point. It helps that which stinks to be turned into rich compost from which new life can grow.

Not only do individuals have shadow selves, but whole nations do too in their shared equivalent of the personal unconscious. In Britain I am convinced that we blundered our way into war in Iraq and Afghanistan – two invasions for twin towers – substantially because we have never dealt with our national shadow left over from the days of the Empire (including Ireland), two world wars, and the Cold War.[38] As John Buchan wrote in 1913:

> Reflect, and you will find that the foundations are sand. You think that a wall as solid as the earth separates civilisation from barbarism. I tell you the division is a thread, a sheet of glass. A touch here, a push there, and you bring back the reign of Saturn. . . . Modern life is the silent compact of comfortable folk to keep up pretences. And it will succeed till the day comes when there is another compact to strip them bare.[39]

When people ask me what they can do about these our troubled times – poverty, war, climate change – my reply is: do whatever you can do outwardly, and as Slim Whitman put it over in the Ned Miller lyric when I was a boy, "Do what you do do well"! But most important of all, do it alongside doing your inner work.

That way we start to integrate the ego self, through the shadow self, into the Godspace of the deep Self. And Jung tells us why this is so demanding, but also, so life-giving:

> If you imagine someone who is brave enough to withdraw all his projections, then you get an individual who is conscious of a pretty thick shadow. Such a man has saddled himself with new problems and conflicts. He has become a serious problem to himself, as he is now unable to say that they do this or that, they are wrong, and they must be fought against. . . . Such a man knows that whatever is wrong in the world is in himself, and if he only learns to deal with his own shadow he has done something real for the world. He has succeeded in shouldering at least an infinitesimal part of the gigantic, unsolved social problems of our day.[40]

The Transpersonal Basis of Community

Now we can glimpse what community perhaps really is, for as the English metaphysical poet John Donne, wrote in 1624: "No man is an island, entire of itself; every man is a piece of the continent, a part of the main . . . Never send to know for whom the bell tolls; it tolls for thee."[41] In other words, wittingly or unwittingly we are bound up in one another at the most profound ontological level.

This is captured in the colour *Plate 4*, which suggests multiple depths of connection in the transpersonal psyche. It is based on Jolande Jacobi's representation, to which Jung himself gave approval.[42] What I like is that it acknowledges the rich diversity of outer difference between people and peoples. It allows for individuality, tribe, culture and ethnicity. But it also shows that if we dive deep enough, there's always an underlying basis for overcoming the problems that such differences can cause.

The bottom line is the central energy of the Spirit that animates all life. It quickens every soul, replenishing libido in the widest sense of that word.[43] Here is the grand unification principle of the psyche. The more we centre into this Godspace, the more that the God-shaped hole of our existential angst fills up. As an ancient Hebrew poet put it, with "goodness and mercy . . . my cup runneth over".[44] Our capacity for spiritual intimacy deepens like a coastal shelf. As the African principle of *Ubuntu* puts it: "I am because you are." It is this love that makes us one another's keeper. This ability both to walk alone and yet, to know communion, that is the foundation, and the fruit, of community.

The Cycle of Belonging

The metaphysical map set out here charts the terrain by which we can become more and more alive to the aliveness of life. It entails overcoming the deadness of apathy. The Greek root of apathy – *apatheia* or *a-pathos* – literally means 'freedom from suffering'. But the shadow side of that freedom can be to find ourselves 'without feeling'. Indeed, this is the normal usage of the word.

Creating community therefore means learning to share feeling; both in its joys and in the burdens of suffering. This implies developing the capacity to *respond* to others. That word comes from the Latin verb, *respondere*, and from it we derive *responsibility*. As such, the cultivation of responsibility emerges as a core dynamic in rekindling community.

I have expressed this in *Plate 5, The Cycle of Belonging* – which is derived from observation of how it is that communities of place find life. Its starting point is the recognition that we all find ourselves in a this-worldly state. Whether in a local sense, globally, or preferably both, we are all incarnate in our bodies, in bodily needs, and in place. Even if we feel 'displaced', we still connect with places every time we eat food, drink water or breathe air. Any person who doubts that they have a sense of place should simply go outside on a clear night and raise their eyes. We don't just have 'somewhere to stay' – we also *live* there, both locally and cosmologically.

Place is a very warm word. It brings together the human and the environment; culture and nature. Awareness of this generates a *Sense of Place*, which is our grounding on Earth.

From here, Sense of Place contributes powerfully to a *Sense of Identity*. Who we are is, in large measure, influenced by where we come from, where we are now based and from where we draw our sustenance. At a very practical level, this is where things like farmers' markets, vegetable box schemes and local energy initiatives are important. Combined with due awareness, they can help to rebuild our uncertain modern connection with place, places, and their people, plants and animals.

Such a Sense of Identity embodies relationship. Inasmuch as we are conscious of it, it builds part of our ego. And inasmuch as we can exercise choice as to which parts to own or disown, it is (like much ego identity) in the realm of the 'head'.

But Sense of Identity is never neutral. It stands or falls on account of the *Sense of Values* that it encodes. These come from the deeper realm of knowing that is the 'heart'.

Once activated into consciousness, values are not neutral either. For the heart pumps blood to both the head and the hand. As such, the Sense of Values stimulates a *Sense of Responsibility* – the capacity to respond. By motivating action – the 'hand' dynamic of Patrick Geddes' 3-Hs – this feeds back into sustaining place and therefore, our Sense of Place.

If we accept this model, we can see that community degeneration comes about by damaging the Cycle of Belonging at any point. Conversely, community regeneration comes about by reinforcing it.

We have now completed our metaphysical exploration. We have seen how epistemology and ontology relate to what a human being arguably is. We have suggested that community is the human ecology that brings together soil, soul and society. From that, we have derived our Cycle of Belonging and seen how this can offer meaning and direction in generating the responsibility necessary for community regeneration. Such is the antithesis to all forms of nihilism.

I have focussed thus far on building a body of theory because we need that to cultivate shared psychospiritual literacy. In these first three chapters I have explored the inner dimension of this and taken matters as deep as I can in prose. But such reflection has to work hand-in-hand with action. In the remaining two chapters let us therefore take a more prosaic turn. It is time to turn our glance outwards. In so doing we will look first at the rural, and then at urban and corporate aspects of regeneration.

Chapter 4

The Rubric of Regeneration

Scotland's Land Reform

This chapter explores community in the context of rural regeneration. It focuses mainly on land reform in Scotland, but in drawing out what I will call the 'Rubric of Regeneration' I trust that the reader will find its implications to hold a much wider geographic validity. I will bring to life many of the points being made using quotations from the WWF-CHE scholars' research, synopses of which have been threaded through this book.

Seven of the WWF-CHE scholars undertook projects related to rural communities. These are summarised in the case studies by Chriss Bull, Isabel Soria Garcia, Rutger Henneman, Iain MacKinnon, Sibongile Pradhan, Mike Price and Jamie Whittle. The quotations used below are taken either from their academic theses, or from their published work as cited in their case study profiles.

As I have described in *Soil and Soul*, land reform is an issue that I became involved with after coming home from the South Pacific. In 1991 I was invited to become a founding trustee of the Isle of Eigg Trust by Tom Forsyth, a crofter (a tenanted smallholder with a share in the common grazing) from Scoraig in the far north-west of Scotland. My interest lay in mounting a challenge to the wider pattern of rural land tenure. Just a thousand owners controlled nearly two-thirds of the private land in Scotland. In those days it was commonplace for landed power to levy unreasonable charges, control and even tax people's businesses, restrict the supply of housing, prevent access and, as a bottom line sanction, to effect summary evictions. Added to that, landlordism exerts a tax on living that transfers resources from the relatively poor to the relatively rich under the euphemistic name of 'rent' or its capitalised equivalent caused by speculation in land values.

The Eigg Trust started off having no money, but a manifesto full of strong ideas (see *Box 13*). By asserting a moral claim of right, we succeeded in spoiling the private market for the 7,000 acre (3,000 hectare) estate. Eventually, after a nail-biting six-year campaign in which local residents progressively took over full control of the Trust, the islanders bought their land into community ownership and did so at the knock-down price of £1.6 million. This sum came from 10,000 donations, and it is worth mentioning in gratitude that 70 percent of them came from outside Scotland – mostly from England.

Other communities followed suit. Political momentum grew, and in 1999 land reform became the flagship legislative programme of the newly restored Scottish Parliament. This led to the passing of the Land Reform (Scotland) Act 2003. It affirms the people's 'responsible right to roam' over nearly all private and public land, including canoeing and overnight camping. It gives rural communities the right to conduct a pre-emptive purchase at government market valuation of any local land that comes on the market. And in areas that are formally under crofting tenure, it confers the right to exercise a community buyout at any time, irrespective of whether the landlord wishes to sell.[45] As of 2008, this 'hostile purchase' provision has never had to be exercised. Its very existence in statute seems to render the lairds (as big Scottish landowners are known) remarkably obliging.

The net result is that from just a tiny base 10 years ago, we now have some 200 communities with varying degrees of community land holding. These account for well over a third of a million acres – more than two percent of all Scottish land. Buyouts are typically followed by the provision of social housing, rising school rolls, new businesses, habitat regeneration and renewable energy schemes. For example, the population of Eigg has risen by 25 percent and has now reached 80 and growing. On the Isle of Gigha, which was directly inspired by Eigg, only one house had been built in the previous 30 years of land-lordism. Now 30 houses have gone up – many with protected tenancies or freehold burdens to stop them being sold on as holiday homes.

The principle of community land ownership is that it makes people tenants unto their own democratically accountable collective selves. Typically, most land will be leased. The community thereby

Box 12: Sibongile Pradhan

Regeneration beyond Land Reform: deeper engagement with community and place in the women of Eigg

My Research

My research was an inquiry into deeper engagement. I wanted to explore what extra intangible ingredients there might be for effective community regeneration in ways that engender a sense of responsibility for community and environment. Drawing on the work of Manfred Max-Neef within an action-research framework, I listened to the experiences of women of Eigg as they raised and reflected upon key issues in community development. These included belonging, responsibility, empowerment, democracy, sense of community, knowledge of self, sense of place, multiple ways of knowing, the feminine, and transformation.

Whilst land reform has now proven to be a key step towards regeneration for many communities in Scotland, the structures in place have so far often fallen short of fully addressing fundamental human needs holistically. For example, there is need for deeper integration of such issues as community cohesion, power dynamics, having a voice, being able to contribute and working through conflict. In my research I was curious to find out more about what it is that gives life, and to explore the unmet needs and aspirations of a remote Scottish community in the light of how regeneration might help to redress them.

My Findings

Through talking with women on Eigg, many of the vital, less tangible, and often spiritual elements of community regeneration were uncovered. They condensed down to three areas. These comprised community regeneration through recognising:

Box 12: Sibongile Pradhan *(continued)*

- a sense of connection with place, the land, the earth, or nature (a spirituality of place);

- a sense of connection to each other (a spirit or spirituality of community);

- a sense of connection with self, and perhaps with 'God' (a spirituality of the whole individual).

Spirituality was understood as being about connection, about knowing and living the interconnectedness of all that is. For the purposes of the inquiry spirituality was often described as that which gives life, that which brings physical, mental and emotional wellbeing, and that which brings out our humanity.

I found that when those less tangible needs for personal, community, environmental and spiritual well-being are not met, there is not just an absence, but in fact a situation of dysfunction. In the course of identifying their unmet needs through stories of woe and strife, the women were on a journey that could transform satisfiers of fundamental human needs that failed, and ended up draining life, into satisfiers that enhanced it.

The research suggests that participatory engagement (encompassing the spiritual, without necessarily calling it that) can strengthen connection, and can help inquire more deeply into and provide a foundation from which to address fundamental unmet needs common to many individuals and communities. My findings also suggested that the way forward is to align policy, structures and local-level capacity building through deliberately developing connection to place, self and community. This calls for a nationwide commitment to real participation and deep engagement.

Next Steps

The process of carrying out this research was a powerful learning journey for me. It was a time of mental, emotional and spiritual growth, and the unfolding and becoming continues. I have returned to the broad field of community development with a deeper, more holistic sense of how to do my work. Through the process of my inquiry I have come to acknowledge and embrace the essentiality of the 'spiritual' in regeneration work. I have also experienced how the role of people in communities can be strengthened through an action research approach. Living life as inquiry has become a daily aspiration.

benefits from its own rents and it also controls the wider infrastruc-
ture, which may also serve freeholds that are interspersed. As a resi-
dent on Eigg put it to WWF-CHE scholar Mike Price:

> There's no need to own land [privately] as long as one can have control over the
> use of the land within reason. . . . You've always got the land; and land is power,
> land is control.

Land Liberation Theology

People often feel that their bond with the land is 'sacred'. In England
this plays out in William Blake's fine hymn, *Jerusalem*. In Scotland the
'soul' element has held prominent place, even in a secular age, alongside 'soil' and 'society'. Interviewed by WWF-CHE scholar Rutger
Henneman, the Eigg Trust's founder, Tom Forsyth of Scoraig,
described how he sees this spiritual backdrop:

> In the Old Testament it's taken for granted that the Earth is the Lord's and the
> fullness thereof. We're not owners, but custodians for a period. Yeah, for me, it's
> just what I call natural justice. It's built into my whole spirituality, my 'being'. [It
> is] a right to have some claim without being ripped off by someone owning the
> land, or owning a right to your labour.

My own position was frequently articulated in the mass media. The
following is an example from a half-page article published in 1996 by
The Herald, one of Scotland's newspapers of record. The fact that the
broadsheets consistently gave prominent space to such views shows
that they were certainly not peripheral to the social concerns of the
time.

> Land is central to human freedom, dignity and fulfilment. It represents the pri-
> mary means of production. It is the location in which community is rooted. It
> is that natural nature in which human nature comes to know itself. It is not nec-
> essary to live directly from the land, but it is necessary to live with it or have
> ready unimpeded access to it. A people alienated from this are a people dispos-
> sessed of both place and self. The landlord, seeking to intermediate between
> people and place, is a bit like the worst type of old-style priest presuming to
> mediate the relationship between the soul and God. It is a theft of power. It
> results in disempowerment and vulnerability.

The question of community land rights in Scotland is therefore much more than just the right to plant trees, catch a trout or be free from egotistical lairds. It is the question of who we are, what we are, where we are in history and how we as a people are struggling to articulate the fullness of our humanity. To those Scots who retain a strong Christian perspective, it is central as the land ethic of Leviticus 25 suggests to the vision of "life and life abundant" of John 10:10. Indeed, there is a Persian saying that when we get to the Pearly Gates, the first question God will ask is "What did you do with the land that I gave you?" [46]

As political pressure for land reform grew in the late 1990s, several of the mainstream churches organised committees or conferences to explore the theology. I believe that these played an important legitimising role for the process in the Scottish psyche. Dr Alison Elliot was at the time Convenor of the politically influential Church and Nation Committee of the Church of Scotland. Her words closely echo several others amongst the 15 'key land reformers' who Rutger Henneman interviewed for his WWF-CHE project:

A lot of people are involved in land reform who would not have said they were religious in their commitment, but there was a deep sense of connectedness with the land; a sense that the land was something that was beyond ourselves. And the theology provided a way of articulating that. . . . The Earth belongs unto the Lord. The land itself is a gift from God. We are stewards of it and we have it in trust. And the idea of somebody 'owning' it in the same way you own a bicycle is something that is deeply offensive to people who have that basic perspective on life and creation.

Not only did theology help to legitimise the movement as it has done in Latin America and elsewhere. It also influenced our methodology. For example, I frequently used and spoke about Walter Wink's approach of (see *Plate 7*):

- Naming the Powers that Be, to expose the abuse of power;

- Unmasking the Powers, to reveal how they cause oppression;

- Engaging the Powers, seeking redemption – spiritual transformation – as the Powers are called back to their own, higher, God-given vocation. [47]

Also important was Paulo Freire's notion of 'conscientisation' – the raising of conscience and consciousness about the dynamics of oppres-

Box 13: *Manifestos of the Eigg community land trust*

"When a shoot is grafted on to an established stalk, the green of the shoot must meet the green of the stalk. The green, or cambium, is the only living and dynamic part of the plant.

"In the cultivation of human beings the same natural law must apply. The Trust aims to be one small step towards the reapplication of this law of nature in human culture!

"Although the Trust's present focus is the island of Eigg, it is hoped that this new concept of land ownership and management could serve as a model where appropriate in other parts."

– Manifesto of the original Isle of Eigg Trust, July 1991.

"To secure the Island for Scottish and global heritage, to be run in the interests of the community allowing security of tenure and sustainable economic livelihood. To encourage continued growth of the cultural heritage and maintain and improve the built environment whilst conserving the ecology of this unique and beautiful island so that it may be enjoyed and shared by all."

– Declaration by residents, 16 July 1994, on accepting full control of the original trust prior to restructuring into The Isle of Eigg Heritage Trust, a charitable company limited by guarantee.

"I would like to add that the Crofters Commission is very conscious of the role you have played in the restoration of Scoraig as a secure community, with a great deal of positive experience to offer others in the Highlands and Islands." – A civil servant's letter (2008) to Tom Forsyth of Scoraig, founder of the original Isle of Eigg Trust, pictured here on Eigg in 2005.

sion. Speaking from his experience in Brazil, Freire pointed out things like: "The oppressors, who oppress, exploit and rape by virtue of their power, cannot find in this power the strength to liberate either the oppressed or themselves."[48]

In this respect the family dynamics of landed power are often unhappy. In her groundbreaking study of women landowners who had been sent away to boarding schools as children, WWF-CHE scholar Chriss Bull concluded that landowning and the social control it gives can be a substitute for having more authentic human relationships. One aristocrat, speaking with what Bull describes as "painful insight", said:

> I hide behind my animals and my commitment to the farm – I think having such an affinity with animals is about having a defect in one's personality – it's compensating for a lack of human relationships.

At the opposite end of the social spectrum, Iain MacKinnon, a young bard and piper who is indigenous to the Isle of Skye, interviewed 14 elders from his home community – all over the age of 50 and half over 70. These revealed the depth of the social scar left by the 19th century Highland Clearances (when landlords decimated communities to make way for commercial farming and blood sports). They testify to the ongoing impact of the modernity that followed. Nobody wants to go back to the hardships of the past, but there was a profound awareness that modern ways have been socially destructive. His key informants made indicative statements like:

- We lived for one another. We worked for one another, and we cared for one another.

- The community had to hang together or it wouldn't work. We just did it naturally. I suppose there is less necessity for it these days. People were so interdependent. I just accepted that.

- What you are is your community. You absorb a lot from your landscape and an awful lot from the people you live with. You might not be aware of it at the time – you might even scorn it – but you are absorbed in it. . . .

- You could probably measure being a Gael in terms of money. If you have up to such and such an amount of money then you are a Gael. Beyond that you are less of a Gael. Maybe it was the fact that people were more on the same level that allowed them to get on.

- I think that crofting, as I knew it, is dead, but what we can show the rest of the country is how to live together as a community. Our society seems to have forgotten how to do that.

In giving a people's condition voice like this simply by having learned how to listen, Iain's work embodies what the great Peruvian liberation theologian Gustavo Gutiérrez calls the doing of "theology from the underside of history".[49] That is to say, it helps communities to become conscientised to ontological issues via their own telling of their own history. This was the process that helped drive land reform in communities like Eigg, Assynt and Gigha. In the case of Skye, Iain is currently exploring how such revitalised connection between the elders and a younger generation can be converted into policy recommendations for the community's future wellbeing. As such, conscientisation pedagogy and liberation theology become eminently practical tools of community regeneration.

The Rubric of Regeneration

The link between social history and present-day liberation is both political and personal. By bringing together the past and the future in the crucible of the present moment, a community undergoes what I call 'cultural psychotherapy'.[50] The elements of this I call 'The Rubric of Regeneration' (*Plate 6*). This expresses the dynamic whereby at all points in the Cycle of Belonging we need to help one another to *re-member* what has been dismembered, *re-vision* how things could alternatively be, and then organise to *re-claim* what is needed to regenerate the community.

Almost always such re-membering will raise issues of intergenerational social trauma, just as personal psychotherapy frequently has to deal with longstanding patterns of family dysfunction. As such, to work deeply with the dynamics of community we must build the skills necessary to recognise and process conflict and violence. Violence within communities takes many forms. We see it in alcohol abuse, apathy, depression and in the emptiness so often at the core of landed power itself.

In understanding this I find it helpful to think about the 'Spiral of Violence' put forward by the Brazilian liberation theologian, Dom Hélder Câmara.[51] He suggests that Level 1 or primary violence is structurally embedded in all manner of social injustices. This stimu-

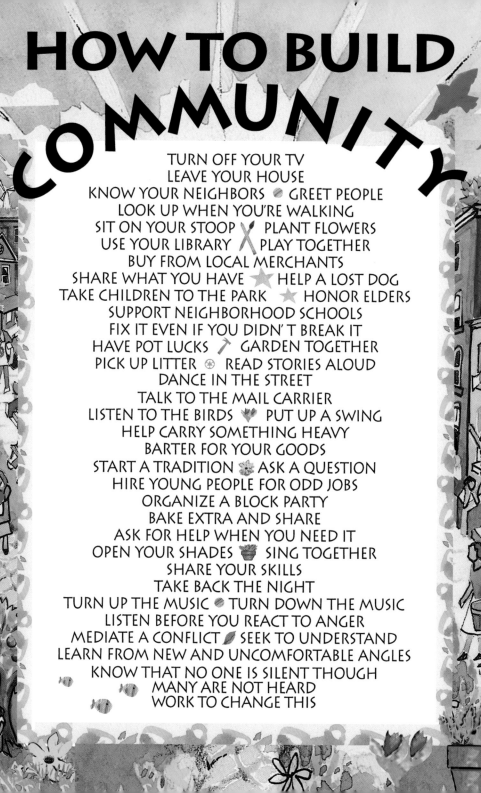

Plate 10. Our schoolgirls in PNG, 1979 - 'integral human development' shows in people's faces.

Plate 11. Andrew Kauleni of SPATF (second from left) at a ferro-cement watertank workshop, Karama, PNG, 19

Plate 12. Village bakery with SPATF's coconut-fired drum oven, Karama, Gulf Province, PNG, 1984.

Plate 13. The GalGael out in their birlinn on Glasgow's River Clyde. *Photo: Barnie Whyte, 2007.*

Plate 14. The author (centre) with Shaun Ferry and Ronnie Latham, GalGael workshop, Govan, 2008 – www.galgael.org. *Photo by generous courtesy of Kirsty Anderson of The Sunday Herald.*

lates secondary violence, which is revolt by the oppressed. The Powers that Be then protect their interests by invoking the tertiary violence of repression. That leads to further all-round impoverishment and therefore to more primary violence. Deep community regeneration must seek to name, unmask and engage to de-escalate this spiral. Peace can become a reality only if justice is established.

Schumacher underscored the importance of working at this depth where he said: "'The Proper Use of Land' poses, not a technical nor an economic, but primarily a metaphysical problem." (7:102)

I have observed that in most Scottish communities that have achieved land reform, the next most important task that follows is to acquire skills in handling conflict. Landlordism often kept a tight lid on the simmering pan and gave the populace a common 'enemy'. Folks never had a chance to develop a full range of competencies for getting on with each other. Once a community buyout lifts the lid, people need quickly to learn that while conflict is normal in human affairs, it has to be recognised and processed if things are not to boil over. Yet again it is a question of constantly naming, unmasking and engaging the Powers that Be – even our very own Powers that Be! In my opinion this requires training for community leaders. In particular, there needs to be an understanding of ego dynamics and the ever-lurking propensity for shadowstrike – the projecting out onto others of unresolved inner conflicts.

If we don't rise to the no-nonsense "tough love" that is needed to face and tackle conflict in our community organisations, then we fall prey to self-destruct syndromes heralding inefficiency. The feminist political scientist Jo Freeman named one such syndrome "the tyranny of structurelessness". Here power denied becomes power abused because people have confused legitimate authority with authoritarianism.

Another syndrome is 'rebels without a clue'. Here the glory-seeker hijacks a ride in the slipstream of others, perhaps exploiting egalitarianism to assert power incompetently. In my view, such narcissistic egotism needs to have its shadow side deflated by "sitting in the fire" (as the psychotherapists Amy and Arny Mindell say). That means robust confrontation. At the same time, as Ram Dass advises, "Do what you have to do with people, but keep your heart open to them." Such problems are best avoided from the outset by having good organisational gate-keeping. I apply what I call "the photocopy test".

Box 14: Mike Price
Meta-motivations and Micro-enterprise under
Community Land Tenure

My Research

Like in many parts of Europe, Scottish community regeneration policy places strong emphasis on job creation – getting people back to work, but often without taking into account qualitative considerations that give people a sense of meaning in their lives. My research sought to examine work from a qualitative standpoint. I wanted to understand what aspects of running a business on the Isle of Eigg gave meaning to entrepreneurs' lives. Was work seen mainly as being for individual 'self-maximisation', or was it also pursued for a wider vision of community benefit?

I carried out my fieldwork over a three-week period using semi-structured interviews and participant observation. Eigg was chosen because of its pioneering and iconic status as a model of community land reform. It has allowed several new business enterprises to emerge since the buyout in June 1997 through the Isle of Eigg Heritage Trust – a unique partnership between the island's residents (50 percent), Highland Council (25 percent) and the Scottish Wildlife Trust (25 percent).

Box 14: Mike Price *(continued)*

My Findings

Manfred Max-Neef's theory of Fundamental Human Needs was used as a framework for analysis. The general consensus was that the people I interviewed were not interested in getting rich. One respondent stated: "I never worked out whether I was making a profit because I was worried that I would find out I wasn't and then have to stop, and if I didn't know then I wouldn't have to stop!"

Through the lens of classical economics this approach to running a business would be irrational. However, traditional economics fails to grasp the importance and hidden benefits of community.

It is the connection between the individual and the wider community that links spirituality to community development. This begins, as one respondent put it, by "acknowledging that the well-being of the individual influences and is influenced by the well-being of the community."

Other interview responses hinted that qualitative aspects of work gave meaning to people's lives in ways that fulfilled them on a deep level such as could be described as 'spiritual'. Values expressive of this included the opportunity for creativity, participation in a cohesive community and an expansive sense of freedom.

Next Steps

Initially nothing was published from this research. The researcher had been affected in such a way that his academic ambitions were abandoned for the time being . . . so that he could start a business of his own! However, a short paper 'Meta-Motivation and Microenterprise on the Isle of Eigg' will now be appearing in Issue 48, autumn 2008, of *Scottish Left Review*.

Offer a newcomer boring but important work like doing the photo-copying. See whether they over-promise and under-deliver, or under-promise and over-deliver. Usually that's an effective self-deselect mechanism!

Still another syndrome is what I heard a priest refer to as "God gets what man rejects." This is the principle whereby right-on organisations act like magnets, attracting those for whom the mainstream world lacks patience. Often I've seen NGOs agonising over the question: "just how many people with 'issues' can we afford to carry?" We all have our 'issues', but the bottom line is that you have to weigh up helping your helpers with what you're all there to serve. That demands frequent discernment. Politics is about engagement with power, but in community we must develop a no-nonsense eye of compassion if we are to wise up to doing our community politics better.

Working with women on Eigg, WWF-CHE scholar Sibongile Pradhan observed that spirituality – that which gives life – can play an important role in building the courage to handle such complex community pressures. In her MSc thesis she describes how:

> The women mentioned a range of things which give life – family, music, land-scape, gardening, sense of God – but mostly it is the land/landscape and sense of community. It was often hard for them to distinguish between the two. . . . Many commented on the island's healing energy and I suspect that the island's role remains key, but in its constancy it is easily taken for granted. . . . I found that it is the community itself which is often felt to be the spiritual core or foundation of the islanders' lives. That which gives life is family and community, i.e., relationships. . . . So much of what made them sad or angry or disillusioned was [when] they were not getting life or nourishment from the community. One woman said she would forgo the other life-giving aspects of island life, such as fine views, clean air or beautiful garden, in order to find community that did not drain, but nurtured and was a wellspring for individual and community growth.

In the decade following their buyout, the people of Eigg have pioneered the handling of such tensions. Neighbouring communities now seek help and advice from them. But we should note the paradox in what has just been quoted. It was precisely from within the community that resources arose to help address the challenges that community had thrown up! Exactly the same is often true of psychodynamics at the personal level. At the end of the day, we each have to dig from where we stand.

Moving to the south of Eigg, Holy Island off the Isle of Arran has been owned since 1992 by a charitable trust controlled by Buddhists from the Kagyu Samye Ling Tibetan Centre. Working in association with the International Union for the Conservation of Nature, WWF-CHE scholar Isabel Soria García concluded that:

> On Holy Island it is understood that any successful conservation has to be based on deep philosophical conviction. Therefore, the spiritual development of all human beings is enough for conserving nature. However, spirituality by itself is not a valid tool for conserving nature. In order for formal protection to come from people and from their experiences with nature, we still need management tools, science and action. . . .

In *Small is Beautiful* Fritz Schumacher remarked: "Where people imagined that they could not 'afford' to care for the soil and work with nature . . . the resultant sickness of the soil has invariably imparted sickness to all the other factors of civilisation." (7:107) Isabel's study shows that management, science and action can integrate in service of the sacredness of place. It takes all three Hs – head, heart and hand – to inform the Cycle of Belonging. Bringing them all together is how both physical and metaphysical reconstruction is made possible.

WWF-CHE scholar Jamie Whittle has now published his thesis about the human ecology of his home bioregion as a book, *White River*. It deservedly went quickly into second printing. His vision of deep ecology – the integration of psyche in wild nature and human nature – leads him up to the one-pointed awareness of the trickle that is the river's source, and then back down again on a journey by canoe that becomes the poetic surge of the whole world. I can think of no better way to close this chapter than with the exquisite beauty of these words:

> I consider the River Findhorn a sacred place. . . . I dream of a day when the watershed of the River Findhorn has been reforested, when the howl of wolves can be heard on moonlit winter nights, and when wild salmon return to the river in abundance. Because that day will be a great day. It will be a day when we human beings have come to see our true place in the interconnectedness of the world, and have been moved to act upon that consciousness. It will be a day when we start to inhabit the Earth with a grace. Like a river.[52]

Chapter 5

Satisfying Fundamental Human Needs

Buoyancy of the Human Soul

Grace 'like a river' is what flows from community in its triune nature – grounding with the environment, with one another, and in the divine. Middle East traditions know grace as the 'water of life'. It flows from under the holy of holies and sustains the leaves of wondrous trees which 'serve for the healing of the nations.'[53] Only from such a standpoint that gives life could Schumacher speak with such authority of "economics as if people mattered". Only from here could he both see and denounce what we're left with in its absence – "the idolatry of economism" (7:112).

In a magnificent essay 'Real People in a Real Place', from a collection fittingly called *Towards the Human*, Iain Crichton Smith, an isle of Lewis poet, shares what it means to see another person as if they actually mattered. He reflects on people who have become uprooted from tight-knit rural communities of place, and he says:

> Sometimes when I walk the streets of Glasgow I see old women passing by, bowed down with shopping bags, and I ask myself: "What force made this woman what she is? What is her history?" It is the holiness of the person we have lost, the holiness of life itself, the inexplicable mystery and wonder of it, its strangeness, its tenderness.[54]

Govan, to the west of Glasgow, is a place where such old women daily shuffle along the streets. The tide has gone out on what was once the epicentre of Britain's imperial shipbuilding industry. Not much remains except for the fabrication of warships. What was once a community of skilled artisans has become one of the poorest urban native reservations in Europe. In the postcode zone where my wife Vérène and I have lived for the past four years – a nice street in an otherwise hard-pressed area – there is five times the national average rate of hospital admissions for drug abuse and seven times the rate for alcohol abuse.

What drew us to Govan was a community regeneration organisation, the GalGael Trust, of which I am a board member and treasurer. It was started by my close friend, the late Colin Macleod and his wife, Gehan, in 1997 with the hope of liberating 'the buoyancy of the human soul'. Colin would say: "You can hold a person down for a long time, but sooner or later they'll come back up again."

Three of the WWF-CHE scholars worked with the GalGael Trust – Brian Thom McQuade, Sam Harrison and Chris Adams. Their findings shed a rare light on the spirituality that can help to redress urban deprivation.

CHE-WWF scholar Brian McQuade was born in Govan's now-demolished 'Wine Alley'. It was one of Glasgow's most notorious slums, but also a community. Brian interviewed 59 local people in his study, the findings of which were subsequently used by Oxfam. Exploring the idea of the Cycle of Belonging, he asked:

> Does the feeling of 'belonging' to a place help to build a sense of identity? Will it carry with it an awareness of values, which inspires a sense of responsibility? Would this then complete a positive feedback – back into generating a sustained and restored sense of belonging?

Brian uses people's real names throughout his report. He insisted that they wanted this. It is part of a culture where people address their life issues in community one with another. In the GalGael we therefore usually don't offer confidentiality, but we do offer respect. Here is how Brian describes a fairly typical interview.

> When Angela Farrell came to live in Glasgow, at the age of 26, she and her husband started a buying and selling business from catalogues which became quite successful. Both of them began to drink heavily and to inject heroin. When the profits from their business were gone, she started buying and selling drugs to feed both their habits, and also to fraudulently claim Social Security benefits. She got caught at this last, and was punished with six months in jail for petty

Box 15: Osbert Lancaster

Values and Legitimacy: responsible purchasing at the Scottish parliament

My Research

In 2003 the Centre for Human Ecology was contracted by the Scottish Parliament to produce a report and recommendations for policy on social responsibility in purchasing.

This led to the adoption of a Responsible Purchasing Statement of Principles which reflects the parliament's underlying values and a commonly recognised articulation of sustainable development. In doing so, the parliament publicly committed itself to a number of ambitious goals including: integrating all issues impacting on people and the environment in the present and the future; and, in selected areas, being at the cutting edge of developing emerging practice in response to social expectations.

My Findings

We started the project by listening to staff. What came across was not only a commitment to professional ethics of integrity and fairness, but also strong personal values of social and environmental responsibility which staff were keen to apply at work.

The decision whether to adopt the Statement of Principles was made by a committee of Members of the Scottish Parliament (MSPs). It needed to be clear to the MSPs that responsible purchasing – as we were developing the concept – was an appropriate objective for the parliament. We therefore linked our recommendations to strategic priorities and existing commitments, in particular to the UK's various commitments to sustainable development and to the parliament's principles of accountability, accessibility, openness and responsiveness, as well as its commitment to equal opportunities.

This created an environment where the Statement of Principles was adopted because of its alignment with organisational objectives, which in turn gave legitimacy to the values and aspirations of individual staff members. Completing the virtuous circle, staff's values reinforced their commitment to the organisation's objectives.

In this project we did not set out to explore the role of spirituality. Indeed, given the sensitivities that the word often arouses, introducing the concept into the project might well have caused major difficulties. However, in semi-structured interviews, the issue of personal values came up naturally: there was a clear appetite among many staff members to find ways to apply their personal sense of environmental and social responsibility in the workplace. Linking responsible purchasing with the organisation's principles created the opportunity for this to happen.

In light of the recent upsurge of awareness and concern about social and environmental issues in general, and global warming in particular, this work suggests one approach to moving from awareness to action: create safe spaces for people to explore personal values, give 'permission' to bring values to the workplace, and make links with wider societal goals.

Next Steps

In my consultancy practice, now with Footprint Consulting Ltd, I continue to apply, develop and test this approach, alongside evaluating clients' impacts, and integrating environmental, social and economic objectives into their organisational strategy. The research described here has been published as Osbert Lancaster and Kyla Brand, 'The Four Dimensions of Responsible Purchasing' in Jonker J. and de Witte M.C. (eds.), *Management Models for Corporate Social Responsibility*, Springer, Berlin 2006.

fraud. When she came out of jail she divorced her husband and decided to change her lifestyle by joining the GalGael Trust as a trainee. One reason was that she likes joinery, while another was that too many of her friends had died through their addictions and she wanted to do something to help her own addictions. Her last reason for joining up and working with the GalGael was that she felt accepted in a place where no one thought of her as 'scum' and where she is treated as a person with a sense of identity.

The core GalGael programme is called *Navigate Life*. Our people work with natural materials – wood, fibres, stone – and in so doing reconnect elementally with fire, air, earth and water. In practical terms it means that a young drug addict, somebody just out of prison, and just ordinary members of the community come into our workshop and are offered a hammer and chisel. They're helped to make something of beauty – perhaps a simple carving of a totem animal, a chest to store belongings or a small table. This deepens their understanding of what Patrick Geddes called "folk, work and place". In a context where food is regularly prepared together, it awakens an ethic of service.

Some help to build traditional wooden boats and sail them out from the River Clyde. Boats for us are more than just objects. They are metaphors for the journey of life – what Joseph Campbell called "the hero's journey" – with its *departure* in youth, *initiation* through the rapids of life where courage is built, and the eventual *return* that draws a person into eldership within their community.[55]

Brian's report concludes that the GalGael's programme clearly strengthens and where necessary, helps to repair participants' sense of identity and belonging. It leaves many feeling "that they had some sort of an obligation to give something back to the wider community around them." He says:

> Normally, when the social cohesion between members of a community and their local authorities break down, people turn to party politics, but here . . . the idea is not just to have a 'sound mind in a sound body' in the community sense, but also to have an individual spiritual and meaningful life where our previous attitudes and concerns will change – particularly our level of confidence, thoughts, feelings and attitudes towards ourselves and the others around us.

Tick-the-Box versus Spiritual Bravery

CHE-WWF scholar Sam Harrison undertook his study with some of the statutory agencies engaged with regeneration in Govan. Whereas GalGael's way of working is akin to that of shamanic cultures with their concept of 'calling back the soul', Sam found, perhaps not surprisingly, that such approaches were (with the important exception of some individuals) off the mainstream's Richter scale. Speaking as a philosopher by original training, he wrote:

> What we see when we experience the violence of cultural destruction, the separation of the healthy from the unhealthy, the human from the natural, and the community from the earth, is nihilism, because it is closed to the reality of life.

Remarking on this, Colin Macleod's wife, Gehan, spoke of what she called 'spiritual bravery' as the essential ingredient for community to become rekindled. On reviewing a draft of this text she emailed back explaining:

> To me it means the bravery to live between what are traditionally held to be 'right' or 'wrong' – to live in truth which can be uncomfortable, scorned or misunderstood. And to deal with the rough as well as the smooth – to cross boundaries without fear of the consequences or perceptions of others.

In her interview she told Sam:

> Part of the reason why the regeneration industry has been allowed to continue this long with little progress to show for the amount of money poured in – is largely down to the tick-box culture that is handed down from above. . . . In worse-case scenarios, it can permeate through the organisation until the whole thing becomes some kind of cynical, tick-box driven, output-obsessed machine, processing disadvantaged people like units in a factory.

WWF-CHE scholar Chris Adams worked with GalGael participants to facilitate the writing of a poetry collection, *Fight or Flight?* Serving regularly as a volunteer sweeping the workshop floors, he built trust in a safe space where spiritual bravery could be explored and then verbally expressed (*Boxes 5 and 6*). Gehan's foreword hints at what urban regeneration looks like when it attends to the inner needs, and not just to the outer economic ones, of real people in a real place.

Box 16: Samantha Graham
Awakening to the Bigger Picture: epiphanies that result in corporate responsibility initiatives

My Research

As a designer and facilitator of experiential ecological education, I wanted to understand more deeply the learning processes of exemplary 'green' managers, in the hope that some of their awakenings to the unsustainable state of the planet could inform management education. The corporate sector has the power, expertise and resources to make a significant difference in restoring the planet and the communities with whom they interact. Often however, the will is missing because the worldview perpetuated in the corporate sector is generally blind to these 'externalities'. I therefore searched for managers whose blinkers had been removed, as evidenced by their industry-leading practices in either ecological or social arenas. Using a qualitative, inter-disciplinary approach, I explored *how they learned* that this bigger picture was important and that it could/should be part of their remit.

My Findings

Two distinct groups emerged amongst the managers, with significant differences in their management practices and discourse, their identity and epistemologies.

Those whose innovations were at the 'environmental management' end of the spectrum, used the language of compliance and risk minimisation to describe their achievements, while their identity was conveyed as fixed, independent and in control. They were managers first and foremost, and there was absence of any passion regarding their environmental work. The separation of humans from Nature implicit in their narratives mirrored the notion that managing the environment is simply an extension of other forms of management with its implicit use of 'power over' whatever is being managed. If one considers the power of self-censorship in conforming to corporate norms, this implies a potentially oppressive treatment of self, including feminine aspects of self and others. Most managers in this group operated from within the unspoken assumptions of the dominant paradigm, pushing on the boundaries, but not questioning them too strenuously.

In contrast, those more at the 'ecological responsibility' end of the spectrum, described themselves in far more fluid terms. Whether re-visioning their sense of self in relation to life because of mystical or religious experiences, or re-construing the purpose of organisations in terms of social responsibility, these managers were very at ease with a less definitive understanding of reality and with their own emotional connection to their work. Their discourses were unusual in the face of conventional business-speak, including notions of service, moral imperatives, personal epiphanies and higher or spiritual purposes. For most there was the sense of a power from within or above that was sacred and that gave them faith or direction when needed. Their innovations were more visionary, less incremental and had further-reaching impacts, social and ecological, than the first group of managers.

In both groups, the manager's identity reinforced their particular ways of knowing, which in turn reflected their managerial language and practices. For example, conventional managerial language reinforces a one-dimensional identity amongst managers and in a mutually reinforcing way, limits the ways of knowing available to management. In contrast, managers who have a more multi-dimensional sense of self, (if they feel confident enough to 'reveal' in the workplace) appear to have access to a greater repertoire of ways of learning, and thereby utilise a greater range of managerial practices, including those incorporating values, ethics, and personal and corporate responsibility.

Next Steps

Building on this research, I design and facilitate corporate sustainability programmes based on human ecology and adult education principles. The aim is to engender a more relational worldview and reduce the work/home division in managers' sense of self, thereby tapping into the power of their deeply held beliefs, passions and desire to make a positive difference. By combining a basic understanding of the science with appeals to participants' emotional intelligence, they are encouraged to replace the practices and language of compliance with those of vision and legacy. The courage required to do this is greatly assisted by the building of community and the willingness of executive staff to lead and support the necessary cultural transformation.

Fight or flight – one of the most basic human instincts – hanging on in a fight for survival in our modern world. We need 'rites of passage' to learn how to temper and shape these instincts so that they serve us rather than rule us, so that we might serve our community. Colin was strong on this – he always said: what alternative rites of passage has our society created? your first stint in jail, your first experience of being chibbed [stabbed/slashed]. For many, GalGael will be a life-affirming rite of passage – that initiation into what it means to be fully human in this world.

Fundamental Human Needs

In working with the notion of becoming 'fully human' it helps to have suitable tools and guidance. One approach is the excellent *Training for Transformation* set of materials from southern Africa.[56] My wife, Vérène Nicolas, uses these alongside a framework of exploring fundamental human needs that was developed by Chilean economist Manfred Max-Neef. Our simplified version of this in the form of a wheel for use by individuals and groups, including the GalGael team, is given in the colour *Plate 8*. We find it invaluable for helping people to weigh up what their fundamental needs are, how adequately each is satisfied, and whether the means of such satisfaction conflict with or synergise with one another.[57]

Workshop participants are invited to shade in the segments of the wheel to reflect how far each need is met. Once the diagram is complete, participants can be asked: "If this was a bicycle wheel, what kind of a ride would you be having?"

People can also be invited to think about what synergises and what violates in relation to particular ways of satisfying a given need. For example, the granting of planning permission for a casino in the name of urban regeneration may create a certain type of economic wealth for certain interests, but it will violate other fundamental human needs in the wider community. By contrast, a social enterprise may see less cash flowing through its doors, but its activities will probably synergise with such needs as participation, understanding, identity, creativity and affection.

The spokes on the wheel can even be scored out of 10. This can be useful in situations where qualitative evaluation requires some quasi-quantitative bolstering. For example, back in my South Pacific days the Solomon Islands Development Trust used a similar approach – it was called the Development Wheel – in deriving a Village Quality of Life Index. Different needs were given a weighting and then added up to produce a crude score – very crude, as it meant adding up things that are not alike – the old methodological problem of apples and oranges. However, it proved useful in targeting development resources, especially in the emergency that followed Cyclone Namu in 1986.

Just as we saw how both science and the sacred are central to conservation on Holy Island, so hard-headed economics and fundamental human needs must also be made to work together. This leads us to government and business, and the place of community in that realm of our lives.

Corporate Social Responsibility

Fritz Schumacher was not naïve about the importance of business and industry to human life. As economic advisor to the National Coal Board he played a pivotal role in one of Britain's biggest enterprises. But today the free market has collapsed much of what the industry was. Whether we like it or not, capitalism rather than nationalised industries provide most of what we consume.

We can either deny this fact or engage with the corporations. The argument for engagement is to raise the level of the field on which their competitive game is played. After all, that game is the sum of our purchasing decisions. If we are honest and look into the corporate mirror it is our own faces, in fair measure, that are reflected back. To this extent we all share some responsibility for cultivating corporate social responsibility (CSR).

If CSR is to mean anything beyond the marketing ploy of 'greenwash', it must be matched up to the yardstick of all-round community. For as Schumacher put it (Epilogue:289):

> In the excitement over the unfolding of his scientific and technical powers, modern man has built a system of production that ravishes nature and a type of society that mutilates man. . . . This is the philosophy of materialism, and it is this philosophy – or metaphysic – which is now being challenged . . .

He goes on to say that "'the logic of production' is neither the logic of life nor that of society. It is a small but subservient part of both." And he is explicit that spiritual values are the only way in which to

Box 17: Wayne Visser
Work in Sustainability as a Path to Meaning:
values and self-transcendence

My Research

My research looks at how work in corporate sustainability contributes to the overall sense of meaning or purpose in the life of sustainability managers. Hence, it uniquely brings together the two areas of corporate sustainability and existential psychology. The research method was to obtain qualitative data from 42 in-depth interviews with 30 South African sustainability managers conducted between 2004 and 2006. The findings contribute to the very limited academic literature on individual managers as agents of change for sustainability, and provide insights into the motivation and satisfaction of sustainability managers which can be applied to the recruitment, retention and management of corporate sustainability professionals.

My Key Findings

- Values alignment (the sense of congruence between personal values and sustainability work) and societal contribution (improving the governance, social, environmental and ethical conditions in society) are among the most frequently cited and discussed sources of satisfaction for sustainability managers. This lends some credence to the idea that these managers are motivated by their personal values and trying to make a difference through the positive impact of their work on society.

- For some managers, their religious or spiritual beliefs are strong drivers for their sense of meaning in life. However, this is not universally the case, and for

Box 17: Wayne Visser *(continued)*

some managers religion was a source of negative or frustrated meaning (this was often linked to the perceived complicity of the Church in social injustices like apartheid in South Africa).

- The findings provide further evidence for the business case for sustainability, mainly through the human resource benefits (managers and staff engaging with sustainability issues are more motivated and satisfied in their work), as well as supporting the moral case for sustainability, i.e. that taking action on sustainability issues based on ethical principles or basic values is both justifiable and likely to be supported by most sustainability managers.

Next Steps

I have used the research to develop a Purpose-Inspired Leadership model, which I deliver as part of the executive learning programmes of the University of Cambridge Programme for Industry. I find the approach of addressing the relationship between 'meaning' and sustainability goes down well with practitioner audiences, since it is more universal and inclusive than 'religion' or 'spirituality', even though they deal with similar issues. I am planning to write a book based on the research, as well as publish several journal articles and Cambridge Research Papers and Thought Pieces.

temper "the egocentric interests of man". But what does this mean for the busy manager at the sharp ends of production and procurement?

For a manager at the sharp end of competition, noble ideals can usually be factored in only inasmuch as they translate through to competitive advantage. But there is a watershed issue here. Each manager has to decide if they're going to encourage the raising of standards, or if they're going to evade and lobby against them. We all have to tread difficult ground along the ridge of valleys obscured by clouds. None of us is uncompromised, and few can be sure of where they're going. The question is: which side of the watershed do you stand on? If everyone walked their lives as you do, what kind of a world might we have? That's the pivotal issue.

Three of our CHE Fellows connected with the WWF scholarship programme have worked on such questions: Samantha Graham, Osbert Lancaster and Wayne Visser. In his study with Kyla Brand carried out for the Procurement Team of the Scottish Parliament, Osbert Lancaster found that the Parliament sought to position itself as follows:

> There was keen interest . . . among procurement professionals leading to the following shared objectives: to create an overarching approach to guide treatment of other ethical and social considerations such as fair trade, employment practices and local supply, to promote compliance with current and possible future regulation, and to improve results through more complete risk management in supplier relationships.

Both Samantha Graham and Wayne Visser found many encouraging examples of individuals doing likewise in corporations. Few executives pretend that this is going to change the world suddenly or radically. CSR against a competitive backdrop has got to proceed by increments, and only green totalitarianism could argue otherwise. As such, CSR may not do a lot to reduce consumption, but it can at least help to change it towards directions that are less damaging.

Wayne Visser undertook much of his research while based in South Africa. An executive who was "somewhat typical" of his interviewees told him:

> It's helping people, it's empowering people, because it all falls under sustainable development, it's ensuring that our environment is taken care of and our kids can be able to appreciate what we have, it's assisting in poverty alleviation, it's getting the business social conscience on the map and on the agenda.

Another said of sustainable development: "When you stand back, it becomes like a religion, it's a value system, it's the way you think about things, and to actually make the first move requires this leap of faith." That leap, said yet another interviewee, required considerable personal commitment:

> You find yourself having to fight the battle of the community against organised industry, because it's the powerless against the powerful. So you find yourself in between, so that actually motivates you because there's a cause. You can, while within a corporate, you can strive to change it, for the benefit of the bigger masses who are poor.

Based in Australia, Samantha Graham had very similar responses from executives selected specifically for their commitment to CSR. She described finding:

> . . . a group of managers [who] inhabited what I call the Whispered Discourses subject position. Their innovations involved both eco-efficiency and eco-effectiveness . . . however their learning experiences tended to take them to less material understandings of themselves and their work. Whether re-visioning their sense of self in relation to life because of mystical or religious experiences, reconstruing the entire purpose of organisations in terms of social responsibility, or connecting passionately with a felt calling, these managers were very at ease with a less definitive understanding of extant reality and/or with their own emotional and ethical connection to the work they do. Their discourses were unusual in the face of conventional business-speak, including notions of service, moral imperatives, personal epiphanies and higher or spiritual purposes.

Such managers were careful to recognise that "the status quo in business does not yet permit language or motivations" that acknowledge their values. This accounts for the necessity of 'whispering'. In spite of this, these managers were convinced that their approach contributed significantly to social and ethical cohesion in their organisations. As Samantha puts it:

> . . . Several talked about the high levels of emotion they had experienced as they learned about the need for, and implemented, their ecological initiatives. One was deeply moved by feedback from his staff that suggested the ecological consciousness-raising he had initiated had greatly affected them, and how grateful and proud they were to be part of the company. This fed into subsequent management decisions.

There we see the bottom line of what can drive corporate change. Unless doing the right thing has positive spin-offs, the company making the effort will not survive competitive pressure. But equally, the more that customer awareness rises, the more a lax attitude to ethics will count against a company. In this respect I remember addressing a seminar at INSEAD, the European business school near Paris. One of the speakers related a conversation with a senior executive from Nestlé. He'd been asked what effect the baby milk boycott of the company was having.

"Very little in economic terms," the executive replied:

> . . . but it makes it harder to attract and hold good staff. They get jobs with us, but then go home, and people say: 'What? You're working for Nestlé? Do your friends still talk to you? Do your children still love you?'

As Schumacher told the world, Buddhist economics is about trying to live our lives in right relationship. If an action damages the web of life, we should turn and think again. If it sustains it, then all are blessed.

At the end of the day, community regeneration is about creating win-win situations. These are the synergies of Manfred Max-Neef's fundamental human needs. It takes practical skills, people skills, and as we have seen in this book, something of a metaphysical leap of faith.

As such, the rekindling of community is not an agenda for the faint-hearted. At its heart is the need for courage. Such is spiritual bravery.

Conclusion

And so we arrive at the end of our short study. It will have become clear that spiritual bravery means that community holders – the elders that we are progressively summoned to become – must deepen in their strength as individuals. There are many seeming paradoxes here. Community involves being, doing and having together. But it equally needs boundaries that can be semi-permeable, a balance between freedom and responsibility, and space between the supporting pillars to respect what Thomas Merton called "the sanctuary of another's subjectivity".[58]

True community can never be about herding, or being mindlessly subsumed into a conformist or cultic mass consciousness. The vanquished perhaps *submit*, but lovers only ever *surrender*. The one implies going under, being subsumed; the other, surfing high on a freely given yielding to the fullness of life. To have life abundant we must become *great lovers* in every sense of that expression. That is the vocation to which we are called – both in and through the experience of community. That's the G-spot!

What a gift Fritz Schumacher's *Small is Beautiful* has been in pointing us to this conclusion! Yesterday's world mainly explored his message about appropriate technology. Tomorrow's world must additionally embrace the metaphysical imperative. Only when the space between outer and inner life is lubricated can community be kindled.

Self-realisation is not rocket science. It's just about getting real. Become yourself. Be yourself! Draw forth the same in others. If in doubt about what to do with your life, feed the hungry – either directly or metaphorically. Start by inwardly asking for the spiritual vision and the courage to work with the shadow. Then step into the ever-deepening beauty that goes beyond both skin and ego. This is the great work of humanisation. This is the soul.

Such a journey winds through space, time and beyond. Gradually the small dream of our anxiety-filled little lives awakens to the pacific vision of the great. Our Hebridean poet said it all. This is about "the holiness of the person . . . the holiness of life itself, the inexplicable mystery and wonder of it, its strangeness, its tenderness." This is membership one of another – community of soil, soul and society.

Alastair McIntosh
Govan, Scotland, 2008

References and Endnotes

1. E. F. Schumacher, *Small is Beautiful*, Abacus, London, 1974.

2. See www.wwf.org.uk/core/ge_0000004945.asp and Tom Crompton's *Weathercocks and Signposts* report, 2008, at www.valuingnature.org.

3. *Liklik Buk* (the Little Book) was published by the Melanesian Council for Churches, 1977 (see Box 4 on page 31 of this book).

4. See Alastair McIntosh, 'Wokabaut Somils in Sustainable Forestry: New Hebrides to Old', *The Tree Planters Guide to the Galaxy*, Reforesting Scotland, Edinburgh, No. 4, 1991, pp.5-7, online at www.alastairmcintosh.com/articles/1991_wokabout.htm.

5. I have posted an extract from Bernard Narokobi's *Melanesian Way* at www.alastairmcintosh.com/general/resources.htm.

6. Catalogue and permissions: www.syracuseculturalworkers.com.

7. The Margaret Thatcher Foundation disputes the order of the wording, and its wider context is not without wisdom. See www.margaret-thatcher.org/speeches/displaydocument.asp?docid=106689.

8. From the introduction to John Lorne Campbell's *Highland Songs of the Forty-Five*, John Grant Publishers, 1933, as quoted to me by the contemporary Gaelic tradition bearer, Norman Maclean of Govan.

9. James Frederick Ferrier, *Institutes of Metaphysic: The Theory of Knowing and Being*, Elibron Classics, USA (facsimile reproduction of the 1875 third edition, Blackwood, Edinburgh), 2005 (originally 1854), p.561.

10. Aristotle, *Metaphysics*, 988a:30-35; 994b:15-20 as in Richard McKeon (ed.), *The Basic Works of Aristotle*, The Modern Library, NY, 2001.

11. Jean-François Lyotard, *The Postmodern Condition: a Report on Knowledge*, Manchester University Press, 1984, p.24 and Foreword at p.9.

12. A. J. Ayer, *Language, Truth and Logic*, Penguin, Harmondsworth, 1961, p.61.

13. Jean-Paul Sartre, *Being and Nothingness*, Routledge, 1969 (originally 1943), p.615.

14. Sartre, *Being*, p.440.

15. Sartre, *Being*, pp.613-15.

16. Evelyn Underhill, *Mysticism: The Nature and Development of Spiritual Consciousness*, Oneworld, Oxford, 1999 (originally 1911), pp.27-31.

17. See Richard Rohr FM, *Radical Grace*, St Anthony Messenger Press, Cincinnati, 1995.

18. Luke 12:49, NEB.

19. Ferrier, *Institutes* , pp.522-5, my emphasis.

20. See full account in Part 4 of George Elder Davie, *The Democratic Intellect: Scotland and her Universities in the Nineteenth Century*, EUP, Edinburgh, 1961, pp.253-338. Aytoun's skit is at pp.294-7.

21. Ferrier, *Institutes*, pp.505-6.

22. Ferrier, *Institutes*, p.252.

23. Abraham H. Maslow, *Toward a Psychology of Being*, Nostrand, Princeton, 1962.

24. George Steiner, *Real Presences*, Faber and Faber, London, 1989, p.227.

25. Matthew 4:1-11; Mark 1:12-13 and Luke 4:1-13.

26. Fyodor Dostoevsky, *The Karamazov Brothers*, Oxford World Classics, Oxford, 1998, Book 5:5, pp.309-32.

27. Matthew 5:8.

28. Dostoevsky, *Karamazov*, Book 6:3, pp.404-5. See the basis of this in Orthodox theology in Olivier Clément's wonderful work, *The Roots of Christian Mysticism*, New City Press, London, 1993, pp.296-307.

29. This definition evolved mutually in discussion with my friend and WWF-CHE scholar, Iain MacKinnon.

30. Philip Boardman, *The Worlds of Patrick Geddes: Biologist, Town planner, Re-educator, Peace-warrior*, Routledge, London, 1978, p.224.

31. Aldo Leopold, 'The Land Ethic' in *A Sand County Almanac: with Essays on Conservation*, Oxford University Press, New York, p.189.

32. Ferrier, *Institutes*, pp.253-4.

33. Some of the best material on this is books and tapes by Fr Richard Rohr FM.

34. Paul Tillich, *The Courage to Be*, Yale Nota Bene, Yale, 2000. For cross-cultural perspective, see Darrell Addison Posey (ed.), *Cultural and Spiritual Values of Biodiversity*, United Nations Environment Programme, Intermediate Technology Publications, London, 1999.

35. Galatians 2:20.

36. See the splendid introductions by the translator, Juan Mascaró, to the Penguin Classics editions of the *Bhagavad Gita*, the *Upanishads*, and the *Dhammapada*.

37. Roberto Assagioli, *Psychosynthesis*, Turnstone, London, 1975.

38. See my article on Cold War psychohistory at www.alastairmcintosh.com/articles/2003-cold-war.htm,

39. John Buchan, *The Power House*, Birlinn, Edinburgh, 2007 (originally 1913), pp.31, 33.

40. C. G. Jung, *Psychology and Religion: West and East*, Collected Works 11, Routledge, London, 1958, p.140.

41. John Donne, 'Meditation XVII' from *Devotions Upon Emergent Occasions*.

42. Jolande Jacobi, *The Psychology of C.G. Jung*, Routledge, London, 1968. (This is the classic introduction to Jung's thought.)

43. To Freud the libido was primarily the sex drive; to Jung it was a much wider life energy, of which sex drive was only a part.

44. Psalms 23:5-6, KJV.

45. See www.landreformact.com. Also John Bryden and John Geisler, 'Community-based land reform: Lessons from Scotland', *Land Use Policy*, Elsevier Ltd, Issue 24, 2007, pp.24-34.

46. Alastair McIntosh, 'Eigg's chance to buy its freedom', *The Herald*, Glasgow, November 16 1996, p.14.

47. Walter Wink, *Engaging the Powers*, Fortress Press, Mn., 1992.

48. Paulo Freire, *Pedagogy of the Oppressed*, Penguin, Harmondsworth, 1972, p.21.

49. Gustavo Gutiérrez, *The Power of the Poor in History*, Orbis Books, Maryknoll, 1983, pp.169-221.

50. Cultural psychotherapy is the underlying theme of *Soil and Soul*, and I have explored it explicitly in the final chapter of *Hell and High Water*, where I also propose a 12-step programme.

51. Hélder Câmara, *Spiral of Violence*, Sheed and Ward, London, 1971: online at www.alastairmcintosh.com/general/spiral-of-violence.htm.

52. Jamie Whittle, *White River: A Journey up and down the River Findhorn*, Sandstone Press, Dingwall, 2007, pp.117 and pp.112-3.

53. Ezekiel 47:1-12 culminating in Revelation 22:2.

54. Iain Crichton Smith, *Towards the Human: Selected Essays*, Macdonald Publishers, Loanhead, 1986, pp.56-7: online at www.alastairmcintosh.com/general/resources.htm.

55. See Joseph Campbell, *The Hero with a Thousand Faces*, Fontana, London, 1993.

56. T for T's new website is expected to be www.trainingfortransformation.net. See also www.VereneNicolas.org.

57. Manfred Max-Neef, 'Development and human needs' in Paul Ekins and Manfred Max-Neef (eds.), *Real Life Economics*, Routledge, London, 1992, pp.197-213, online at www.alastairmcintosh.com/general/resources.htm.

58. Thomas Merton, *Wisdom of the Desert*, W.W. Norton, NY, 1970, p.18.

Index

crofters and crofting 18, 62-3, 67, 73, 78, 80
CSR (corporate social responsibility) 13, 89, 95, 98-9
CSVPA (Cultural and Spiritual Values of Protected Areas) 25
cultural psychotherapy 80, 106
culture 24, 27, 66, 69, 70, 87
Cycle of Belonging 5, 6, 13, 44-5, 55, 70-1, 80, 85, 87
see also sense

D
Delos Initiative 25
Devil
as *diaball* or *diabolos* 52
the 52-3
discernment 23, 84
Donne, John 69, 105
Dostoevsky 52, 54, 104

E
economics 28, 48, 63
as if people mattered 13, 32, 86
ego, the 26-7, 57, 60-1, 64-5, 71, 102
see also self
elders 61, 66, 79, 80, 101
Elliot, Dr Alison 77
engaging the powers (Wink) 77, 81, 105
environment 3, 21, 24, 30, 70, 74, 78, 86, 88-9, 92, 98
epistemology 35, 46, 55-6, 71, 92
essence 34-5, 38, 42-3, 46, 54, 56
essentialism 13, 35, 38, 42, 46-7
evangelicals 46
Eysenck, Hans 60

F
Ferrier, James Frederick 35, 43, 46, 57, 104-5
folk, work and place (Geddes) 90
Forsyth, Tom 72, 76, 78
Freire, Paulo 77, 79
Freud, Sigmund 65, 105
Fundamental Human Needs (Max-Neef) 83, 86, 94

G
Gaelic and Gaels 32, 66-7, 79, 103
Gaia Coach Institute 13
GalGael Trust 36-7, 40, 45, 50-1, 87, 90-1, 94
Navigate Life programme 51, 90
García, Isabel Soria 6, 24-5, 72
Geddes, Sir Patrick 56
God 20, 26, 39, 43, 46-9, 53-4, 59, 61, 64-5, 76-7, 84
consciousness 64-5
gets what man rejects 84
spot (the G-spot) 43, 47, 101
Godspace 64, 69 see also self, deep/great
Govan 36, 44-5, 50, 86-7, 91, 102-3
grace 43, 85-6
Graham, Samantha 6, 92, 98-9
grounded philosophy 6, 50, 56
grounding 13, 43, 46, 70, 86
Gutiérrez, Gustavo 80, 105

H
hand 51, 56, 71, 85
Harrison, Sam 3, 6, 13, 50-1, 56, 87, 91
head 48, 56, 71, 85
heart 12, 19, 33-5, 38-40, 42-3, 47, 51, 54, 56, 63-4, 71, 81, 85, 100
hearth and fire as metaphor 33, 36
Hebridean Isles 17, 22, 32, 48, 102-3
Henneman, Rutger 6, 58-9, 72, 77
Highland Clearances 79
Highland community 6, 22, 66
history, theology of 77, 80, 86, 105
holiness of the person 86, 102
human
condition 9, 11, 13, 32, 34
needs, fundamental 5, 13, 74-5, 83, 86, 94-5, 100, 106
human ecology 9, 12, 19, 28, 30, 44, 49, 67, 71, 85, 93
as PRED/PRET 30
triune basis of 49, 53, 55

I
idolatry 41-2
individualism 27
Institutes of Metaphysics (Ferrier) 43, 104-5
intelligence 46
interconnection 24, 43
intermediate technology 15, 18, 105 see also appropriate technology
Iona Community 9, 26, 30
Isle
of Arran (Holy Isle of) 6, 24-5, 85, 95

THE SCHUMACHER SOCIETY
Promoting Human-Scale Sustainable Development

The Society was founded in 1978 after the death of economist and philosopher E.F. Schumacher, author of seminal books such as *Small is Beautiful, Good Work* and *A Guide for the Perplexed*. He sought to explain that the gigantism of modern economic and technological systems diminishes the well-being of individuals and communities, and the health of nature. His work has significantly influenced the thinking of our time.

The aims of the Schumacher Society are to:

- Help assure that ecological issues are approached, and solutions devised, as if people matter, emphasising appropriate scale in human affairs;

- Emphasise that humanity can't do things in isolation. Long term thinking and action, and connectedness to other life forms, are crucial;

- Stress holistic values, and the importance of a profound understanding of the subtle human qualities that transcend our material existence.

At the heart of the Society's work are the Schumacher Lectures, held in Bristol every year since 1978, and now also in other major cities in the UK. Our distinguished speakers, from all over the world, have included Amory Lovins, Herman Daly, Jonathon Porrit, James Lovelock, Wangari Maathai, Matthew Fox, Ivan Illich, Fritjof Capra, Arne Naess, Maneka Gandhi, James Robertson, Vandana Shiva and Zac Goldsmith.

Tangible expressions of our efforts over the last 25 years are: the Schumacher Lectures; the Schumacher Briefings; Green Books publishing house; Schumacher College at Dartington, and the Small School at Hartland, Devon. The Society, a non-profit making company, is based in Bristol and London. We receive charitable donations through the Environmental Research Association in Hartland, Devon.

Schumacher UK Members receive Schumacher Briefings, Schumacher Newsletters, discounts on tickets to Schumacher Lectures and Events and a range of discounts from other organisations within the Schumacher Circle, including Schumacher College, Resurgence Magazine and the Centre for Alternative Technology (CAT).

**The Schumacher Society, CREATE Environment Centre,
Smeaton Road, Bristol BS1 6XN Tel/Fax: 0117 903 1081
admin@schumacher.org.uk www.schumacher.org.uk**

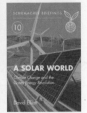

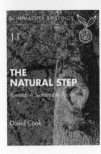
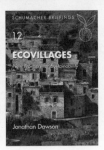

1. *Transforming Economic Life*
   James Robertson £5.00

2. *Creating Sustainable Cities*
   Herbert Girardet £7.00

3. *The Ecology of Health*
   Robin Stott £5.00

4. *The Ecology of Money*
   Richard Douthwaite £7.00

5. *Contraction and Convergence*
   Aubrey Meyer £5.00

6. *Sustainable Education*
   Stephen Sterling £5.00

7. *The Roots of Health* Romy
   Fraser and Sandra Hill £5.00

8. *BioRegional Solutions* Pooran
   Desai and Sue Riddlestone £6.00

9. *Gaian Democracies* Roy
   Madron and John Jopling £8.00

10. *A Solar World*
    David Elliott £6.00

11. *The Natural Step*
    David Cook £6.00

12. *Ecovillages*
    Jonathan Dawson £6.00

13. *Converging World*
    John Pontin and Ian Roderick £8.00

14. *Youth-Led Development*
    David Woollcombe £8.00